# TEACHING U.S. HISTORY AS MYSTERY

# TEACHING U.S. HISTORY AS MYSTERY

David Gerwin and Jack Zevin

HEINEMANN
Portsmouth, NH

**Heinemann**
A division of Reed Elsevier Inc.
361 Hanover Street
Portsmouth, NH 03801–3912
www.heinemann.com

*Offices and agents throughout the world*

The authors and publisher wish to thank those who have generously given permission to reprint borrowed material:

"History as Mystery" by Micah Zevin. Used by permission of the author.

Figure 1–1. Photograph by Iris Zevin. Used by permission of the photographer.

Figure 3–1. Photograph of Annie Oakley in Brooklyn. Reprinted by permission of the Denver Public Library, Western History Collection (call number NS216).

Figure 3–2. Buffalo Bill's Wild West Show poster of "Miss Annie Oakley, The Peerless Lady Wing-Shot" by Nate Salsbury. Reprinted by permission of the Denver Public Library, Western History Collection (call number NS245).

Figure 3–3. Annie Oakley photograph by Stacy, Brooklyn, New York. Reprinted by permission of the Buffalo Bill Historical Center, Cody, WY, Vincent Mercaldo Collection (accession number P.71.361).

*(credit lines continued on p. vi)*

**Library of Congress Cataloging-in-Publication Data**
Gerwin, David.
  Teaching U.S. history as mystery / David Gerwin and Jack Zevin.
    p.  cm.
  Includes bibliographical references and index.
  ISBN 0-325-00398-X (acid-free paper)
    1. United States—History—Study and teaching.   2. Teaching—Philosophy.
3. Teaching—Methodology.   I. Zevin, Jack.   II. Title.

E175.8.G47 2003
973'.0971—dc21                                              2002191304

*Editor:* Danny Miller
*Production editor:* Sonja S. Chapman
*Cover design:* Suzanne Heiser, Night and Day Design
*Composition:* House of Equations, Inc.
*Manufacturing:* Steve Bernier

Printed in the United States of America on acid-free paper
07  06  05  04  03  RRD  1  2  3  4  5

*FOR*
*my mother*
*BRENDA I. GERWIN*

*and*
*my wife*
*IRIS L. ZEVIN*

# CONTENTS

History as Mystery...

Sometimes, I get lost in my own personal Bermuda triangle,
my room, a sinking ship spinning to the oceans bottom or to mythical
Atlantis where the world was once just castles and sand. Or, I'd make pyramids
out of wooden blocks and paper-mache, pretending I was a pharaoh and my
fingers were slaves endlessly building an empire. Some Sunday afternoons,
I'd happen on a war movie on the French Revolution, I'd see Napoleon,
demonstrative, angrily flailing his arms, one hand forever immersed
inside his vest below the lapel, and wonder whether it was there to
keep him warm, was he holding a knife or pistol, or was he
just feeling the pulsating sensation of his heart. Other days, I'd think
about when I was a little child, where I was born and how I got out of the
hospital like a wounded Civil War soldier waiting to heal or be reborn. The only history
I have is the ones my parents have told me—

It is a mystery like the shadow of my early years . . .

—Micah Zevin

# ACKNOWLEDGMENTS

## From David

In the spring of 2000, Nancy Dill, the acting dean of the Division of Education, came to the Department of Secondary Education and asked if anyone wanted to offer an experimental course in an innovative fashion. With Jack's encouragement, I put together a two-week institute, 8 to 4 daily, revolving around the theoretical concerns about practicing history raised in Chapter 2 and many of the case studies developed in other chapters. The staff of the Rosenthal Library at Queens College was gracious in providing a classroom, which made the collections accessible in ways that would not otherwise have been possible. For two summers in a row, students signed up for a course that required them to read several books and write drafts of three papers before the class even met. Why did students take such a course? For some of the students it was the first time they had ever been on the Queens College campus during the daytime, and the first time they had the leisure to use all of the resources of the library. One problem with teacher education, I now realize, is that too much of it takes place late at night while stacks of papers and lesson plans are waiting at home.

The intense nature of the collaboration produced a sense of camaraderie I have seldom experienced in a class. All of them have my gratitude and I want to thank them by name. Summer 2000—Timothy Becker, Roland Cameau, Kate Coughlin, Karen Dillahunt, Lisa Forte, Patrick Frino, Aristotle Galanis, Leonard Geller, Christopher Hammond, Charles Jardines, Brian Kotzky, Chris Leonard, Stephanie Lord, Michael Macklin, Gary Martin, Marc Niebergall, Jennifer O'Brien, John O'Leary, Brenda Perina, Robin Roopchand, Mary Schiller, Karen Snyder, and Patrice Williams. Summer 2001—Tina Baio, William Campione, Alida Cente, Kristin Fraga, Peggy Gorry, Kathleen Jordan, Anna Kostro, Jessica Lopez, Madelyn Roesch, Krista Schmidt, Rebecca Segna, Adam Stonehill, and Jennifer Theo-Kupstas.

During the first summer, more than half the students collected their curriculum units together and copied them, producing a bound volume of all their lessons. During both summers, the class helped field test the mysteries in this book, and I have been fortunate enough to visit the middle and high school classrooms of some and watch people who took my class teach their mysteries. Larry Geller of the first summer's class hosted me over three days as his classes explored the mystery of the Embargo and the War of 1812, material he later presented at a conference on using primary sources.

During that first summer, I used a documentary, *The Uprising of 34*, to demonstrate the "hidden mysteries" that exist in all communities. One of the filmmakers, Judith Helfand, provided me with the film and information on a high school project in Lodi, New Jersey, based on the fading memories of a plant explosion in that community. I hope that the collaboration we began then will continue and deepen. A project she codirects, Working Films, is listed among the web resources at the end of Chapter 6. It helps bring documentaries, particularly about working, to the classroom.

The second summer I taught History as Mystery I used *Uprising* in combination with *Heaven Will Protect the Working Girl*, a video from the American Social History Project (ASHP). We contrasted the documentary with an historically accurate semi-cartoon portrayal of work in a sweatshop and daily life. The ASHP materials that put social history at the center of narratives, and their education programs connecting the CUNY Graduate Center with New York City's public high schools, have made it one of my homes within CUNY.

During both summers, I used the board game Diplomacy (Hasboro) as an example of a mystery approach to World War I. For that idea and some of the readings around it, I am indebted to my friend and colleague Victor Assal. That effort grew into a collaboration with ICONS at the University of Maryland, and a chance to continue working with a student, Charles Jardines, from that first summer's class.

Randy Bomer and Terry Osborne are two former colleagues who have had a big impact on how I write and how I work. Arthur Costigan and Rikki Asher are two current colleagues who have involved me in writing projects. Doug Dixon began teaching social studies education with me at Queens College and has since moved on, but it helped to have someone else trying to figure it all out.

## From David and Jack

Our primary home at CUNY has been and remains the Department of Secondary Education at Queens College. We have had the pleasure of working with a supportive group of dedicated colleagues who live their vocations and make a difference in the life of our students and our city. Some are having a national impact on public education. The entire department has our thanks for their support and encouragement.

Two members of the department, Kathy Nava and Bonnie Willichinsky, had to deal with a History as Mystery course that was scheduled "outside the bounds" of summer school. They fit it into three different rooms since there are no day-long blocks in the master schedule, kept the course on the summer schedule for 2001, and handled a million other details that made it possible to actually hold the class. Without their continuing efforts the department would come to a halt.

Anne Marie Nava provided crucial technical assistance in printing an Apple file on a Windows machine, while retaining the formatting.

Julie Savarese is one of three students in the last five years who attended the MS program in social studies at Queens College as a full-time graduate student. It is hard to realize that one year ago she was a college senior. A gifted educator, she started doing a bit of work with us, and during the fall, she began working as though she was our doctoral student. There is other research she conducted with us that we hope will appear in print elsewhere. For this book, she took charge of requesting permissions and spent hours researching images for use in different chapters. We miss her now that she has graduated and is teaching high school. She has already demanded the chance to write a chapter of her own if we get as far as a second edition.

Heinemann has provided us with two editors, Bill Varner who developed this project with us and left before it was finished, and Danny Miller who has seen us through to the end. Bill listened to our ideas for this book and led us through a revision of our proposal that produced a much clearer and stronger conception of history through mystery. Danny has been the rare editor who can see the forest while pruning individual trees. Each sentence has benefited from his guidance.

We would be unable to undertake a project of this scope without the pre-existing research others have carried out and published. We acknowledge the generous assistance and sympathetic support of professionals such as Ranger Robert Palmer of the Effigy Mounds National Park and his colleagues at the National Park Service, the Smithsonian, state historical sites, and at many museums and historical societies. Although not every mystery we researched has been included in this edition, they made it possible for us to obtain original photos, images, and textual evidence, some which appear here. Cinder Stanton of Monticello went a step further and voluntarily provided a close reading with corrections and comments on the entire section concerning Thomas Jefferson and Sally Hemings. She saved us from many errors, major and minor. Her questions made us clarify our questions and our arguments. The errors that remain are ours alone.

## From Jack

Many thanks to the support provided by my long-serving and loyal secretary, Ms. Doris Davis, and my wife and educator partner, Iris, who helped test and refine many of the history-as-mystery lessons for me.

## From David

What I know about teaching history I learned first and best from Carole Powers, high school teacher, then my high school department chair, and always a friend. I am blessed to be surrounded by a warm and loving community of friends, both in the neighborhood and further away. Minyan M'at, the Farm, Bavli-Yerushalmi, colleagues in CUFA, and friends from college and graduate school have all encouraged me in this project.

We are lucky to be close to our siblings and parents. My mother, Brenda Gerwin, is a model of courageous accomplishment. She earned her Ph.D. in biochemistry in 1964. The Nobel-laureates offering her a post-doctoral fellowship announced that she was the first woman they had selected and demanded that she agree not to get pregnant during her training with them. Though she accepted, that was the last significant compromise I heard of, and she has negotiated much of life on her own terms, switching labs and fields to stay near enough to home, learning Hebrew as an adult, retiring when it was time and launching a new program of study. Her recent battle with a potentially fatal illness has again shown me what it means to affirm life at all times. It is with love and a bit of awe that I have dedicated this book to her.

Above all I want to acknowledge my wife, Lisa Gersten, whose partnership enriches every part of my life, and my daughters Mikaela and Yardena who are mysteries that change over time, and are a continuing source of joy.

# An Introduction to a Mystery
# Teaching Strategy

Children, I have always taught you that history has its uses, its serious purpose. I always taught you the burden of our need to ask why. I taught you that there is never any end to that question, because as I once defined it for you (yes, I confess a weakness for improvised definitions) history is that impossible thing: the attempt to give an account with incomplete knowledge, of actions themselves undertaken with incomplete knowledge. . . . I taught you that by forever attempting to explain, we may come not to an Explanation, but to a knowledge of the limits of our power to explain.

—GRAHAM SWIFT (1983, 181–82)

## A criticism of history teaching

Teachers, us included, are often tempted to present history as a list of facts and stories about the past, particularly the names and dates of people, battles, countries, and legislative acts. These facts and stories may be worth knowing for certain special occasions, and to show off erudition, but these tend to be unsatisfying as a steady diet for most students. Facts, so called, are usually connected to ideas—ideas of causes and effects, ideas about truth and beauty, ideas about human decisions and human inertia. One set of facts can help to explain why there was a Civil War, while another set of facts may help to explain the effects of the Civil War. At its worst, this piecemeal approach reduces history to rote memorization, often leaving students bored and indifferent, if not hostile, to a course. At its best, this approach leads students to question what might have happened if the list of facts had been different. But either way, the past is frozen; it is a dead past, someone else's past with all the facts generated by authorities, leaving the student with the problem of stacking them into definitions, categories, causes and effects, and historical theories.

There is very little personal connection with history for students through this largely didactic telling-the-story and listing-the-facts method. Furthermore, there are few opportunities to develop a fascination with history, the art of storytelling, and the complex motivations that impel people to act in historical events. Students, we argue, miss out on the opportunity to think for themselves, to draw their own conclusions, and to take ownership of historical events so that they can write or rewrite stories about history.

## Changing our view of facts

One goal of this book is to change teachers' view of facts as *truth* to facts as *evidence*, evidence that can be used to answer or raise questions and solve mysteries. We prefer the words *evidence* or *data* or *artifacts* because they have an unfinished feel to them that the word *facts* doesn't have. Evidence can be added or subtracted. Data can be stored, accessed, and manipulated. Artifacts are mysterious remnants of the past that must be interpreted. All of these words invite the student to invest meaning into the basic narrative and information they are studying. Students are encouraged to view history as a puzzle—a set of dilemmas, a collection of conflicting viewpoints—in short, a mysterious and engaging subject!

By the end of this book, you as readers, whether teachers or students, should be more comfortable trying to deduce interpretations from evidence; dispute each others' facts; and understand problems involved in the origin, production, and suppression (yes, that too!) of historical evidence. Hopefully, you will have a more flexible notion of history as statements about the past that are *probably*, or most likely, true as our best reading of current evidence rather than settled and final answers. There is also the possibility that what you once saw as proven fact may be far less certain than you had believed to be the case. We will try to convince you that notions about the past are subject to challenge and can change in the face of new evidence, new readings, and new theories, and that old evidence, old stories, can be reinterpreted through new eyes.

## History as mystery

Instead of history experienced as *lists*, this book's readers will experience history as *mystery*. Some mysteries will arise because the evidence itself is mysterious. Other mysteries will arise because we have questions about the past that are not so simply answered based on the kind of evidence that is available. These mysteries have philosophical and value issues embedded in them and may result in a variety of dilemmas. By the end of this book, readers should no longer rely strictly on other people's answers, or even on other people's questions. They will want to know more about the evidence, and readers will want to develop questions of their own. Working through the cases in this book should foster a thorough and fulfilling realization that at ground zero everybody gets to think for herself or himself leaving you in exhilarating, giddy haste to begin thinking about some interesting problem or issue.

It is this spirit of openness and investigation that we want to foster, and which we will assist you to develop through examples of evidence that invite discussion, analysis, debate, and argument. Teaching history as mystery is an attitude as much as a method. It is based on a respect for the evidence of the past, particularly primary sources; a suspicion of the ready-made interpretations of others, even noted scholars; and a recognition that you and your students have ideas to contribute to the process of understanding history.

This book also presents techniques for constructing or *manufacturing* mysteries out of history, and then teaching history as mysteries to middle and high school classes. For students, engagement will be the key, and they will be unlikely to notice the manufacturing process until the end of an investigation. We introduce these techniques through case studies, presenting the evidence for a case and walking you through the steps for solving that mystery. Following the case study, a teaching section explains how to develop similar historical mysteries (including information about obtaining materials) and then makes suggestions for instruction. We will conclude each chapter by briefly reviewing the concepts, the case or cases, and the teaching techniques that build a mystery for students.

### To Do

- Make a list of historical events and personalities in U.S. history that you feel are well understood.
- Make a second list of historical events and personalities in U.S. history that you feel are poorly understood.
- Check those that might present an opportunity for reinterpreting through new lenses, and check some that you see as offering little or no possibilities for new viewpoints. Explain why you made your choices.

## The educational psychology of teaching history as mystery

> Modern pedagogy is moving increasingly to the view that the child should be aware of her own thought processes, and that it is crucial for the pedagogical theorist and teacher alike to help her to become more metacognitive . . . to be as aware of how she goes about her learning and thinking as she is about the subject matter she is studying. Achieving skill and accumulating knowledge are not enough. The learner can be helped to achieve full mastery by reflecting as well upon how she is going about her job and how her approach can be improved.
>
> —JEROME BRUNER (1964, 64)

Mystery is a powerful technique for teaching history because it has certain inherent properties that motivate students. First of all, mystery arouses curiosity. Students who might not care very much about reading history become fascinated when confronted by the problem of sorting out clues and putting together evidence for a solution. According to the theories of teaching and learning we are basing our ideas on, there is a psychology of interest and excitement that comes into play when students are faced with the unknown. It is a little bit worrisome to enter into a world of uncertainty, but it is also very exciting to play the role of detective. The neat trick for a teacher is to *balance* uncertainty against knowledge, and to offer sufficient clues to keep the detectives moving along, but just a little short of frustration and solution.

Second, mystery builds interest because a solution is its own reward. Students must collect evidence, put clues and cues together, sort out the relevant from the irrelevant, and come up with a theory or prediction that is convincing to others. This process challenges students, sustains attention, and encourages investigation in a way that a predigested program or textbook cannot. The reward for a successful student conclusion is intrinsic and does not need to rely on external reinforcement from parents or teachers. A really good history mystery can literally *impel* students to work at completing their investigations and developing their own interpretations. The elements of the mystery draw students into a problem and they, and you, may end up doing far more studying, thinking, and writing than was originally assigned. In short, intrinsic motivation will take over and propel learning.

Teachers can open up history mysteries to students in three major ways:

1. By choosing people, topics, and events that are themselves mysterious or problematical.
2. By purposely creating mysteries using commonly taught historical and social studies materials.
3. By raising open-ended questions about current understandings or misunderstandings of historical people, places, and events.

---

### You Decide

- Write your own theory of student interest.
- When were you ever captivated by a subject? Why?
- When were you really bored by one and why?
- Which sorts of topics interested or bored you, and do you think it will be the same for your students?

---

## Teaching mysterious and problematical events

Topics and events that are mysterious present puzzles to those who want to learn more about them. We can read what is known and reported, but there always seem to be points in the narrative that are confusing, inconsistent, and/or contradictory.

---

Why the United States became a party to the Vietnam conflict can be explained on a number of levels and yet definite reasons elude us when we learn that our leaders were confronted with the very troublesome experience of the country's previous French rulers. Warnings were offered but went unheeded and no one is quite sure why. The United States also seemed to hold on longer than appeared necessary, according to many observers and historians, and then finally withdrew in a rather humiliating debacle. Why? A great classroom problem has just been identified.

Ancient Native Americans, for example, left widespread communities with large earthen mounds throughout the Ohio basin and much of the Mississippi River Valley, but then they disappeared from the scene. These people have been called Mound-builders, Hopewell, or Adena but we really don't know their names, origins, or beliefs. More mysterious yet, no more mounds were created after a certain time, and most, if not all, of the communities had abandoned their towns before Europeans arrived. Furthermore, many of the mounds contained artifacts that are very reminiscent of the Aztecs or other people from central Mexico—communities quite far from Ohio and Illinois. Was long-distance trade quite active during that period? Were migrants from Mexico among the settlers of Ohio? Did Native Americans share similar beliefs from the beginning? On second look, maybe the artifacts aren't all that much like those from Mexico. Perhaps we have overrated the likenesses? Alas, these people exist no more, thus we cannot interview them to discover the answers to our questions so that we can solve the mystery of the mounds' purposes and origins. Therefore we have the makings of a fine puzzle for students to investigate.

---

Both Vietnam and the Moundbuilders are genuine mysteries of different kinds, and it is easy to involve students in discussions and debates about either or both. Many more mysteries are suggested from historical evidence, some of which demand consideration of issues, while others require analysis of archeological ruins. However, the idea of mystery can also be introduced into everyday lessons in which we have a good grasp of origins and meaning. In these cases, the mystery technique can be used to reinvigorate topics that students may find boring or irrelevant. Reconstruction, for example, is often taught as a series of amendments to the Constitution and a few key pieces of congressional legislation. Instead, this complicated moment in our history had witnesses who wrote from so many different perspectives (Radical Republican, Klan leader, Freedmen, etc.) that we can construct a mystery that catches students' attention. Mystery is not only where and when you find it, but also can be planned and plotted for good motivational effect by teachers.

Mystery as an idea and as a teaching technique has a lot going for it because, as noted earlier, it is deeply rooted in human psychology. Human beings, particularly younger ones for whom experiences are fresh, have a natural curiosity about themselves, their family and society, and why people behave or believe in certain ways. Students also have a great need to play, to engage their minds and bodies in games that test their knowledge, skills, and cleverness. A mystery has many gamelike features that challenge us to solve the problem, find the unknown, identify the culprit, point out the weapon, interpret clues, and so much more. In effect, a good mystery is a puzzle, a game, which beckons us to work out a solution, hopefully a successful conclusion.

Our thesis in this book is simply that these deep-set needs and our natural human curiosity can be harnessed by you, the teacher, to stimulate student problem solving. Once stimulated, and sustained, students can be encouraged to improve their observation, reading, writing, listening, and thinking skills almost without need for additional exhortation. The mystery stimulates a whole range of intelligences, if you will, that the student must bring to bear on the problem in order to achieve a satisfactory conclusion.

For you, the teacher, we are arguing that it doesn't matter if students solve the problem totally or not since it is the process itself that is so valuable in building motivation and enhancing learning. Furthermore, the problem may not be fully solvable in a final sense. Thus, students will learn to deal with uncertainties and make inferences that are more typical of real life than are pat textbook solutions to problems.

Mystery is a very powerful motivation and sustained learning force, providing that it is applied properly in the classroom. In terms of human psychology, the value of the mystery should be left largely to students to decide and to complete. Interference by the teacher or an expert or a parent (i.e., giving too many clues, providing answers when students get stuck, or leading students to conclusions) will make it much easier to reach a solution but will kill students' motivation. If the teacher provides too many explicit instructions about the solution or extrinsic rewards, it will be unnecessary for students to complete their own thinking and work out their own theories. A balance is called for in which the people, teachers, curriculum writers, parents, and/or tutors can set the stage for a mystery, but must then allow enough room for students to maneuver searches and infer conclusions.

Thus, mystery can be a metaphor for problem solving, involving several degrees of difficulty and a few different kinds of unknowns that students will encounter and become so intrigued with that they will want to complete the task largely for their own intrinsic reasons. They often become emotionally attached to the problem and will seek a solution, the best one they can find, perhaps with your help, perhaps not. But the will to discover, once formed, drives students to develop an answer to the perceived mystery. At the point where students become engrossed in the problem, we should limit involvement to guidance and encouragement, and hold back on pointing out strategies and answers until much, much later.

Deep involvement in a problem, according to educational pyschologists, produces exactly the kind of systematic and engaged learning that we are hoping for: the kind of learning *how to learn* that students will remember and transferr to other situations.

### You Decide

Use mystery as a metaphor to review aspects of a typical American history program.

- Which events are heavily overlaid with propaganda?
- Which events have hidden agendas?

- Which personalities have been reduced to *cartoons* of human beings and which have been given a lot of space? Why?
- Which leaders have been glorified and which have been vilified: Is there any pattern?
- Where have problems been nicely ironed out and solved for students even when it is clear we really don't know . . . Remember the *Maine*!
- Who started the Haymarket Riot?
- Why did we take over the Vietnam conflict from France?
- Why do we call many conflicts, actions, and revolts *wars* while we call other wars *police actions* or some such?
- Which metaphors are used in some historical descriptions (e.g., conflicts, civil strife, and economic suffering), and which are used in harmonious events such as treaties, labor settlements, and the passage of bills by Congress?
- Can we separate language from events, metaphors from historical understandings or misunderstandings?

## Purposely creating mysteries: Let's hear a cheer for perplexity!

Sometimes, particularly in U.S. history, events, people, and places may be too well-known, too familiar, or too numerous for of us think about. All the facts are there to see but often students are not terribly interested in the story. The ideas presented may be seen as hackneyed and commonplace. The focus on names, dates, and places bores young people, and they exhibit low levels of motivation to carry on with their studies. So, why not purposely reconstruct materials and present them as mysteries to engage student interest? Design lessons to perplex, engage, puzzle, and arouse curiosity.

Constructing a mystery can be easily accomplished by a variety of techniques such as introducing unknowns; deleting names, dates, and places; mixing up sequences; and juxtaposing conflicting viewpoints side-by-side, but without indicating what person is speaking for which point of view. Making history mysterious has many pedagogical advantages. Plainly, when students see data missing or crossed out, they begin to wonder about what is not there. They tend to read assignments much more carefully because of their perplexity. They begin to take a search for clues seriously in order to discover a document's author, time period, setting, or origin. You, as the teacher, can use students' demonstration of careful reading (perhaps aloud on occasion) as a diagnostic tool to learn more about how they approach problems, what they understand, and how good or bad is their detective work.

Mixing up sequences by offering two or three readings or pictures from different time periods, but on the same subject, for example, forces students to compare and contrast the ideas, people, and technologies in each as a first step to identifying the times in which they were composed, drawn, or photographed. Students begin to think about historical context as if they were detectives looking for clues rather than as passive observers who simply have to check the date in a caption or footnote. Setting up disagreements, conflicting accounts, or inconsistent reports attracts attention particularly if the contrasts are dramatic. Students wonder why witnesses can't agree, and how reports can vary so widely. Coming to grips with conflicting reports tends to promote student observational and inferential skills, helping them to develop theories and explanations for the mysteries they discover. The fact that students are rediscovering something you already know in no way detracts from their practice with reasoning through the problem, and it sparks interest in studying history.

- Could you tell the time period of a portrait from the way it was drawn or the pose and clothing of the subject?
- Could you put excerpts from three Lincoln speeches in chronological order just from what he says and how the President says it without resorting to reference books?
- Could you make sense of an old letter that has been partially destroyed and is written in a strange script with many odd spellings of English words?

Real challenges, eh? Well, that is exactly the idea of constructing mysteries for classrooms purposes. These are among the many ideas and techniques we are suggesting you try out in your classrooms to create student perplexity and enhance the motivation to learn history and social studies.

### To Do

Select a favorite and much used, even overused, document of American history to convert into a mystery. A favorite of ours is Abraham Lincoln's famous letter to Horace Greely, which has some very striking lines in it and a big mystery about what Lincoln *really* believed about slavery and the Union. Was he really, deep down, interested in freeing the slaves no matter what, or was he really more interested in saving the Union? What does he say? What metaphors does he use? Which is the *key* line and why?

## Raising open, unusual, and thought-provoking questions, and more

Teachers can introduce a sense of mystery into the most ordinary and standard lessons by raising thought-provoking questions, ones that demand answers supported by reasons, by evidence, and preferably by criteria. Snap answers simply won't address these questions: thought, often a considerable amount of thought, is required of the student to approach an answer. Raising thought-provoking questions is easy, particularly in certain areas of history (e.g., when attempting to link people and events, when identifying causes and consequences, and when trying to evaluate and/or judge an historical person's behavior). Thought-provoking questions usually grow out of theories, careful and detailed observation, or from unusual perspectives.

We might look at a standard document like the Declaration of Independence from a semiotic, sociological, or anthropological perspective and see what we get in the way of new and mysterious questions and answers. What signs and symbols, ideas, and assumptions did the writer of the Declaration make the most use of, and which ones did he avoid and why? How did the author view other peoples and nations? Was his language biased and stereotypical, say, about the King of England? About Native Americans? Why did the author direct most complaints at the King and not at the Parliament, which held the most power in England at that time? Who should have really been blamed? Was the author's language indicative of superior or ordinary status, and how can we tell just from the document alone? With questions like these, you may just be able to rekindle interest in a document that may have been taken for granted by your American history students.

We can find a good deal of evidence of early Americans driving out Native American people, and killing off nearly all of the buffalo that the plains' people depended on for their sustenance. Early explorers, army contingents, and traders also destroyed, or almost destroyed, numerous other species, often with a sense of glee and accomplishment that seems astounding to us moderns who sometimes pay a lot to travel to national parks to see the descendants of those nearly extinct animals. Why did the cowboys and trappers, hunters and herders, many of whom we romanticize now, seem to have such a poor sense of conservation? Were the Native Americans themselves always good managers of their environment? If so, why did so many towns and villages disappear from the Ohio River Valley and the Southwestern United States? Why didn't the explorers or trappers care, or did they really care but were at a loss as to what to do? What are the motives for ecological destruction? Do the same or different motives come into play today when discussing drilling for oil in Alaska, saving the Spotted Owl in Oregon, or opening the California Redwoods area for lumbering?

As you can see, there are questions aplenty to ask from many different perspectives in order to get a discussion going in a history classroom. Constructing questions and encouraging students to answer them, however tentatively, is the beginning of creating intrinsic motivation to inquire on one's own—to be a detective who investigates problems, discovers answers, identifies missing pieces of the puzzle. Creating practice mysteries builds interest and promotes interpretational skills. Delving into mysteries provides students with a heightened awareness of the past as a forgotten place, of the biases and vagaries of historical witnesses. Students become acutely conscious of history as a complicated subject, one filled with intriguing questions, problems, debates, and unsolved (perhaps unsolvable) mysteries. Student consciousness and perspective on history are just what we are proposing as the heart and soul of teaching history. We want the student to slide into time; try to recapture what has been lost; and to rebuild clues, evidence, and artifacts into a new and coherent, but forever incomplete and contestable, record of people, places, and events.

- How do you get involved in the past?
- Which questions do you think are most exciting to you and your students?
- What are the characteristics of an exciting and mysterious question?

## A beginning conclusion

As we work toward building a new attitude for the study of history, we will look for ways to present American history as hands-on involvement, as interpretation, as uncertain in many aspects, and as bringing a sense of mystery. From this base, we hope to prepare you and your students to view the past as negotiable, with the intention of inviting new viewpoints and new meanings.

This introduction provides you with a framework for choosing topics that are mysterious, debatable, and open to questions. In addition, we have offered ways in which you can create a mysterious atmosphere by using engaging classroom strategies and techniques. In Chapter 1, we offer categories for classifying mysteries as minor, medium, and major; and we provide you with a set of instruction guidelines for students based on a philosophy of:

- Shared inquiry
- Utilizing primary sources
- Testing evidence for logic and bias
- Acting as questioner/devil's advocate
- Creating a sense of play and enjoyment.

Each of the cases presented will work out methods for presentation, which you are free to embellish, diminish, or revise to suit your own situation and style. We invite you to apply, use, and revise any and all evidence and questions here and to evolve your own way of teaching history as mystery.

So, let's hear it for teaching history as mystery, whether through real mysteries, purposely constructed classroom problems, or thought-provoking questions. And let's give a cheer or two for perplexity and puzzlement as well!

## Resources

BRUNER, JEROME. 1996. *The Culture of Education*. Cambridge, MA: Harvard University Press.

BURKE, PETER, ed. 1992. *New Perspectives on Historical Writing*. University Park, PA: Pennsylvania State University Press.

COLES, ROBERT. 1989. *The Call of Stories: Stories and Moral Imagination*. Boston: Houghton Mifflin.

GARDNER, HOWARD. 1991. *The Unschooled Mind: How Children Think and How Schools Should Teach.* New York: Basic Books.

HOLT, TOM. 1990. *Thinking Historically: Narrative, Imagination, Understanding.* New York: The College Board.

MOFFETT, J. 1968. *Teaching the Universe of Discourse.* Boston/New York: Houghton Mifflin.

SCHAMA, SIMON. 1992. *Dead Certainties: Unwarranted Speculations.* Cambridge, UK: Granta Publications.

STEINBERG, R. J., ed. 1988. *The Nature of Creativity: Contemporary Psychological Perspectives.* Cambridge, UK: Cambridge University Press.

SWIFT, GRAHAM. 1983. *Waterland.* London: Heinemann.

WHEELER, WILLIAM BRUCE, AND SUSAN D. BECKER. 1994. *Discovering the American Past: A Look at the Evidence, Vols. I and II.* Boston: Houghton Mifflin.

ZINSSER, W., ed. 1995. *Inventing the Truth: The Art and Craft of Memoir.* Boston: Houghton Mifflin.

# 1

# Mystery in History
## Guidelines and Levels of Investigation

Most of the issues mankind sets out to settle, it never does settle. They are not solved, properly speaking, being concerned with incommensurables. At any rate, even if that be not always true, the opposing parties seldom do agree upon a solution; and the dispute fades into the past unsolved, though perhaps it may be renewed as history, and fought over again. It disappears because it is replaced by some compromise that, although not wholly acceptable to either side, offers a tolerable substitute for victory.
—JUDGE LEARNED HAND, 1872–1961 (1952, 281–84)

## What is *history as mystery?*

The idea of mystery implies a search, an adventure, an intellectual puzzle, a tingle of excitement, and perhaps fear, as we leap into the unknown. Deeply embedded into mystery is the notion that we are in possession of only parts or pieces of the whole, and that we need to find clues so that we can understand what has happened. Mystery attracts because it is both a challenge to our intellects and a pull on our emotions. We are never quite sure what we will find out, or whether we will be able to reach a satisfying conclusion.

In short, mystery is humbling. We do not know it all, maybe far from it. Worse yet, we are not certain of our evidence, or able to perfect our understanding, for many and varied reasons. To solve an historical mystery, even partially, the past must be brought back to life. This is, of course, impossible. The best we can do is play with probabilities, test data, and the *best* of that is a conclusion that may come up to *beyond* a reasonable doubt, but never exceed that level of inference.

History, like mystery, must delve into the past for clues and motives. As historians, we must search through words, documents, diaries, news reports, songs, stories, diplomatic accounts, paintings, photographs, and other sources, for evidence, for corroboration, for comprehension, for inference, and for theory. But it is we, not those who are gone, who put the clues together, and we must do so carefully, or we will make serious mistakes about the past and about ourselves. We will fail to grasp what happened and why it happened unless we open ourselves to observation, gathering data, and explanations that help us understand human actions and motives.

As you can guess, finding details in history is not easy, but it is fascinating if viewed as mystery, and a lot more honest than most of the *finished* answers we often settle for when we study people and places from bygone times. Our argument in this book is simple: that history, which is a flawed, partial, and often biased record of the past, can be taught and learned as mystery. Why? For the following two major reasons:

- *First*, because what happened should be viewed as incomplete and problematical, and approached as open to many interpretations rather than just one
- *Second*, because mystery has built-in psychological motivations for gaining student attention and building interest in learning

The popular computer simulation, *Myst*, cleverly combines mystery with history, shrouding events in fog, hiding clues, and providing confusing explanations, very much like real historical study. We see history, the raw stuff, as messy, opinionated, confusing, argumentative, and often lacking sufficient evidence of the kind we need to draw definitive conclusions. Nevertheless, historians, social scientists, and educators draw conclusions all the time and present these to kids as complete—the whole truth and nothing but the truth. This is not entirely honest, we say, because we just don't know for sure a lot of what happened or why it happened. And, if we do think we know it for sure, it is not very interesting to teach because all you can do is tell the students the truth you know so that they can write it down in their notebooks. There isn't much to do anymore!

Therefore, we propose teaching history as mystery to arouse student interest, and to help students understand the tools and methods by which historians and social scientists ferret out answers, if they are able. This method has some simple but thought-provoking rules; as they say, if you want to play the game, know the rules. Here we offer a series of historical detection rules to follow, which may help you become a better observer and investigator.

Throughout this book, we hope to stimulate your thinking about history, mystery, social science, and the arts, perhaps in ways you may not always agree with; but do let us know when you disagree. Keep notes. Write us a letter. Develop your own ways of making history mysterious for your and your students, and share your ideas with us and others.

## Some rules for teaching history as mystery

The whole idea of teaching history as mystery is to get students thinking, really thinking hard, about what happened and about why it happened, about why someone said it happened, and about why we think that person is probably honest or not. That is, we want to hear their ideas; we want to see evidence; and, above all, we want to hear reasons, hypotheses, interpretations, and theories that analyze and explain events. In the process of teaching and learning, we also want to turn kids on to history; promote interest; and get them talking their heads off about sources, witnesses, biases, probabilities, generalizations, perspectives, and emotions.

The next sections describe some suggestions about how to get the history-as-mystery process rolling, and about how to keep it going to achieve some satisfying conclusions about both content and process issues, however tentative and revisable these may be in the future. Above all, the tables of inquiry have to be turned between teacher and students, giving the detective role to the students—they become Sherlock Holmes and we become Dr. Watson, if you will, supportive of their inquiry perhaps, putting on an act that is just a bit bumbling.

## A rule in favor of shared inquiry

First of all, encourage students to learn how to draw their own conclusions and to defend themselves against criticism from other "detectives." In effect, each participant becomes a partner, a team member, in an investigation to which all have a chance to contribute. And contributions, including your own, must be defended and supported by evidence, sources, references, and reasons. You can join in with more suggestions, questions, and pointers, but this must be done carefully so as not to destroy students' sense of independent inquiry. You can intervene, of course, if discussions go very far astray, but this has to be held to a minimum in order for student detective work to proceed in amassing a goodly amount of evidence. Foster distinctions between poor- and high-quality evidence, original sources and secondary or tertiary sources, confusing artifacts and consistently organized artifacts, reliable sources and those that represent a distinct point of view. Help students become conscious of evidence as created and authored rather than simply discovered.

## A rule in favor of raw, unpolished evidence and disagreements among witnesses

Second, give students a quantity of poorly organized and confusing evidence and clues to work with in their investigation. Arrange the materials just as they may have appeared in historical times or in archeological digs. Give them primary sources whenever possible, with the original language and images. Test student understanding of the texts and images by asking for interpretations when they read, hear, and/or see the materials. Sometimes, this may not be practical because old texts are unreadable in their original orthography, because they were written in foreign languages, or because they are very long and complex, requiring editing. But, as much as is practical, offer students a sense of the past by giving them documents, paintings, songs, and such, pretty much as they appeared at the times they originated.

For still more difficult mysteries, provide students with contradictory witnesses. Turn their attention to the age-old problem of which witness is more honest and truthful than the others. Request reasons for their decisions, and inquire as to how they judge honesty and sincerity. Give them "doctored" evidence in which people have deliberately left out what is needed to know a reasonable, balanced opinion. Offer a few theories and explanations for events, and let them in on professional arguments between and among historians and social scientists now and then just so that they know the experts aren't necessarily a lot better off than they are. Experts are often just better informed and in possession of more rigorously organized research methods, but still don't always make a reasonable decision! We can use experts' methods and make decisions ourselves—they might even be better decisions.

## Test evidence for tampering and test everyone's reasoning for logic

Third, keep options open for everyone—you, the students, and the experts too. Negotiate answers between yourself and students, and between students and other students. Have everyone in the classroom join in the process of checking evidence, researching data, comparing and contrasting sources, looking over alternative explanations, and exploring different theories. Develop within-this-rule rules for good solid evidence and for faulty evidence, for sound reasoning, and for sophistry. Discuss the quality of the evidence, its source, quantity, relevance. Aim at critically examining reasons as circular, syllogistic, or incomplete. Introduce students to some critical-thinking techniques. Eyewitnesses, "great" persons, scholarly experts should all be examined carefully so that students don't fall prey to believing ideas just because they are presented by the smart and famous, or by leaders and heroes. No one is exempt from being checked or questioned. Develop a sense that history was "created" by fallible humans who often were intent on serving their own interests and goals, sometimes quite consciously but sometimes perhaps unconsciously. Be skeptical!

## Play the questioner, devil's advocate, provocateur, innocent, ethical standard bearer—Ask, don't tell!

Fourth, serve as an investigator role model by asking students a lot of questions. Ask yourself questions in private while preparing your mystery lesson, and then select the most powerful of these for use in the classroom. Ask the students questions. Ask the students to ask each other questions. Ask questions of authors, of documents, of artists, of scholars, of professors, of historians, of each other during discussion time. Encourage everyone in your history-as-mystery classroom to ask questions out loud, and, of course, leave time for answers and especially for student-to-student conversations and arguments. Focus on teaching students to ask probing questions rather than simple queries for more content, dates, names, and places. Press for questions that ask why and how; that call for contrast and comparison; that zero-in on values, biases, distortions, and propaganda techniques. Develop a set of criteria for lower-, middle-, and higher-level questions with students: Encourage them to differentiate between didactic, reflective, and affective queries, the easy, moderate, and difficult.

## Use mystery to promote a sense of play and to energize a sense of accomplishment

Fifth, have a lot of fun playing with questions, negotiating answers, poking through clues, arguing about explanations, interviewing witnesses, finding solutions, and studying the past. Don't make historical detective activities seem like work, rather deal with the problems as play with a purpose.

Conceptualize work and play in history as closely related: two halves of the same process of learning and thinking. Promote a sense of play in mystery to increase student motivation. Historians often have this sense of wonder and fascination in their studies, but it is masked by voluminous scholarship and carefully defined goals, which students may not be ready for yet. Use the psychology of mystery, the desire to probe the unknown, to solve a problem (even if others have solved it or tried to solve it before), to drive demand for more and better, wider and deeper evidence. In this way, history as mystery may accomplish many of your content goals, but in a way that makes it all seem enjoyable and entertaining rather than plodding and pedantic. Data collection, studying multiple viewpoints, and engaging in argument and debate will sharpen students' work skills in historical inquiry while at the same time bolstering their level of interest in pursuing solutions. This is the basis of teaching history as mystery—inquiry as a mutually supportive combination of work and play, play and work. We propose that the motivation provided by this approach will lead to a better sense of historical accomplishment and enjoyment for most students.

## Defining history as mystery

If we think about history as mystery and mystery as history, a big topic, we need to break it down into some component parts that make it easier to deal with as teachers. We need to look at just what we mean by history as mystery, and we need a set of categories to help us understand which are easy mysteries and which are difficult ones. In an ultimate sense, history is largely unknowable because it has passed and time cannot be regained, at least this far into our technological development in the early twenty-first century. All evidence is partial at best, and deeply biased, or so privileged by our society that we don't even read the evidence anymore (go on, see how many slaves were actually freed by the Emancipation Proclamation).

To even really understand events of the very recent past, we must sort and organize evidence into a new *whole* through which an older context may be recaptured. Some mysteries involve just a search for clues, mementos, and data; others demand more in the way of discerning patterns and developing interpretations; still more call on all of our skills at detecting value orientations and all sorts of bias, evasion, propaganda, self-aggrandizement, ethnocentrism, reconstructions, and historical revisions. These problems in themselves suggest the mysteries of the historical process in which many try to portray themselves and others as better, or as worse, than they probably were in reality. Here is where research, observation of details, cross-checking of sources, critical reading, and a healthy skepticism play a vital role in good historical detective work.

We therefore propose dividing historical mysteries into several categories ranging from those that are easier to deal with through those that present moderate problems to those that are more demanding to solve.

*Minor mysteries*: Fairly easy to understand, provide only a few sources for error, are quick to solve, offer sources that are in agreement, and contain relatively few methodological issues.

*Medium mysteries*: Somewhat confusing evidence, sources for error in both the data and eyewitness reports, require considerable effort to find a solution, contains a number of conflicting viewpoints, and raise investigative questions.

*Major mysteries*: Complex and disorganized evidence, errors arising from data, eyewitnesses, and bias, solutions require extensive effort, multiple contradictory perspectives, and conflicting historical interpretations that generate questions about both the nature of knowledge and the way history is studied.

## Five scales to judge mysteries

As noted before, we are proposing that the problems and historical inquiries that we call mysteries can be judged according to a number of criteria such as difficulty in comprehension, possibility of errors, speed of solution, and conflicts between witnesses and viewpoints. These criteria should be thought of more as sliding scales of questions and solutions for mysteries than as distinct divisions or clear categories. The differences are those of degree rather than kind, based mainly on the complexity of an investigation and the depth of analysis demanded for a sound conclusion.

Thus, you might want to consider conceptualizing mysteries in history as ranging from minor to medium to major, based on the following five criteria.

*Comprehension*: Easy to medium to difficult—Is the data readable, straightforward or confusing, simple, disorganized or complex?

*Reliability*: Few chances for error to some to many—Are there errors arising from missing data, from witnesses' lies and untrustworthiness, or deep-seated biases?

*Viewpoint*: Agreeable to conflicting to contradictory—Do perspectives concur, stand in opposition to each other, or express inconsistent and contradictory positions?

*Solution*: Quick work to moderate to extensive study—Is a little or a great deal of detective work required? Is knowledge missing and discoverable, partially corroborated, or speculative and unrecoverable?

*Issues*: Informational (facts) to interpretation (reasons) to theoretical (historiographical/affective)—Does the mystery raise mainly factual questions, reflective/perspectival questions, or extend to overall questions of meaning, emotions, and judgment?

### Criterion one: Comprehension

Just taking in or understanding an historical mystery may offer problems, particularly if the reading material is old and handwritten in a style with which we and our students are not familiar. Artifacts, which are totally unfamiliar to us, may be involved, making comprehension more difficult. There may be a lot of disorganized material to assimilate, or there may be only a few items to consider. Diaries or letters, written in a personal and user-friendly style, may be a lot easier to understand and interpret as data than official pronouncements, leading us to view the evidence as more approachable, resulting in greater clarity of conclusions.

## Criterion two: Reliability

Error is part of any historical investigation and can stem from any number of causes, including the data itself, the number and kinds of witnesses relied on for information, and the tendency of historians to overlook or overemphasize conditions of factors shaped by their own times or theories. Mysteries that provide sound, but partial, data should probably be considered minor, while those that include documents posing purposeful lies, ideology, and/or biases might be seen as medium or major. The extent and depth of unreliability or trustworthiness of data, witnesses, and historians should shape your rating.

## Criterion three: Viewpoint

Viewpoint deals with the problem of perspective in historical documentation. When all or nearly all evidence points in the same direction and witnesses and historians agree, then clearly we are dealing with a minor mystery. However, when there are conflicts about the evidence itself, about the reasons underlying a series of events, and about overall interpretations by scholars, historians, and leaders, we are faced with much more difficult problems. If there are clear-cut pros and cons to deal with, then the problems, in our judgment, are of a medium level. The toughest cases arise, we feel, when disagreements and conflicts are contradictory and even mutually exclusive, with many different overlapping perspectives in which people cannot agree on the facts, the reasons, or the issues, or perhaps even the way we process knowledge.

## Criterion four: Solution

How much work is needed to investigate a given topic may be determined by the amount and quality of the evidence available. Often, there is far too much evidence, some of which can help you and your students to find a solution, but some of which can obscure important details and causes. We would argue that *missing-pieces* problems, once identified, clearly define the amount of work to be done and that a minor problem is usually faced. Solutions tend to surface quickly if we have many witnesses or sources that corroborate an event. However, if missing pieces are only partially recoverable and only partially corroborated by other sources, corroborated only by single biased sources, or totally unrecoverable, then a medium or major mystery may result.

## Criterion five: Issues

This is even a difficult criterion to explain, but we will try. A mystery may present problems in which the *way* we use facts, interpretations, and/or theories are discussed and debated, leading to disagreements about the nature of historical knowledge. How we use the data of history can be a problem; for instance, what we choose to emphasize or disregard, overlook or privilege. Sometimes choices may be deeply psychological, or influenced by our culture, upbringing, and politics, consciously or subconsciously, leading to conclusions that another person from a different background and culture may find very disagreeable and/or inaccurate. Worse yet, depending on their views of knowledge, scholarship, and political philosophy, historians may disagree about how to handle facts, interpret cause and effect, and defend conclusions. For example, some historians think all evidence is *constructed* (i.e., collected, interpreted, and shaped by one's perspective and society), while others believe that *truth* can be discovered by careful analysis, collation, and corroboration of evidence.

Tough or major mysteries therefore can contain many sources of error and a good deal of suspect evidence, including biased witnesses and contradictory accounts. These errors can result in conflicting historical interpretations, where even the methods of investigation are at issue. Some mysteries, usually minor, are more like a good detective story in which the clues finally come together in such a way that conclusions are beyond a reasonable doubt. In other cases, both the content and the process of study are open to question, leading to dilemmas and paradoxes that cannot ever be fully solved.

## Three levels of historical mysteries

Our proposal is to view mysteries as a series of graduated levels from minor to medium to major, each of which can be judged against one or more of these five criteria, which can be changed by adding or subtracting criteria of your own.

### *Minor mysteries*

Many mysteries in history arise basically from a lack of evidence, overlooked evidence, and poor or unavailable research tools. Accurate data is generally available at the historical time and can be corroborated by witnesses. This data can lead directly to a solution to a controversy or problem. Sometimes the evidence is available but suppressed, hidden, or unusable with current scientific or technological capabilities. At other times the evidence may be overlooked because the politics or culture of the time shifts interest to other topics and issues. Basically, what makes this level of mystery work well in a classroom is searching for missing information—the pieces of the puzzle that seem to have been lost or overlooked. Once particularly useful data is found, or partly or mostly uncovered, the mystery can be declared solved at some fairly high level of probability. However, conclusions may still be overturned some time in the future because there is always the possibility of new evidence about the same subject.

Minor mysteries may be easy to solve if we look for more and better evidence from which to draw more reliable inferences. However, many are harder than they seem to be on the surface since all of the data cannot always be found when we need it or may never be completely discovered, uncovered, or deciphered. So, at best, we may offer easy solutions to many mysteries in history based on our most reasonable conclusions given all the evidence collected. The hope is that these conclusions and interpretations won't be challenged by new evidence, new views, or changing historical modes of interpretation.

Now and then, minor mysteries can grow quite complicated when the evidence being turned up displays a wide variety of viewpoints and/or raises issues of knowledge construction, or reliability of sources are raised. This often happens when written records are scarce, as in archeological studies, or on topics where evidence has been purposely suppressed for political reasons, perhaps by a slave owner, a conqueror, or a new government. Different detectives, perhaps social or biological scientists, as well as historians, get into the act of solving the problem and you find out that there are variations in viewpoints; a number of *whodunit* theories develop as a result. This type of problem, which begins "shading" into a medium-level mystery, can be solved by ranking the many factors (i.e., determining which are most important), and noting which theories put the facts together most elegantly or most efficiently. Then we have a more sophisticated and multilayered solution than would be the case for a mystery that is mainly a puzzle with missing pieces.

## Medium mysteries

Medium mysteries are not as easy to solve as minor mysteries: They take more time and may involve disputed evidence or evidence prone to a number of errors. Such mysteries appear to be only partially solvable because they involve multiple perspectives, disagreements, and perhaps several eyewitnesses with ambiguous or clashing viewpoints. Some evidence and the interpretations that arise from the database may be challenged by relatively simple questions about the cultures and politics of the times, places, and persons that involve meaning and viewpoint issues. For example, events may be emotionally important to the people involved and reporters/witnesses may cast each person or action in a light they consider favorable to themselves or their side. As you can see, this makes it harder to solve the mystery of, say, what really happened than if we are seeking missing pieces that can be collected or researched.

In discussing medium mysteries, both the evidence and perspectives can present problems. Both may contain discernible errors, inconsistencies, and language that is not entirely comprehensible or is purposefully ambiguous. Evidence may be one-sided, with the opposition's view partially missing or destroyed, rewritten, or recollected by outsiders to the events. Perspectives can also present problems since many medium mysteries in history arise from accounts by eyewitnesses or recorders who are passionate about events, passions that often are so strong that we are swept away by them and lose sight of the broader picture. We become, in effect, brainwashed—pulled emotionally by one side or view or belief system—and tend to view others who were involved as primitive barbarian, immoral, disgusting, or even inhuman. This emotional shift may twist or challenge our usual careful procedures for achieving a balanced judgment.

In a medium-level mystery, we often have considerable knowledge, but we can't really explain what happened at a high level of probability, or with only a few errors, because evidence is one-sided or missing, or both. Furthermore, witnesses, reporters, and, perhaps, we ourselves are emotionally involved and can't reason as objectively as we would wish about the issues. As historical detectives, we can try to control the damage by suppressing emotion, factoring out strong viewpoints, lining up opposite views, and searching for more evidence from third parties to the events under discussion and analysis.

Medium mysteries require attention to theory, to historiographical tools, and to ways of thinking, as well as to the continuing search for more and better evidence that characterizes minor mysteries.

## Major mysteries

The deepest and most profound mysteries involve explanations and theorizing about human behavior because even with the evidence we have, and it may be considerable, we still cannot build an adequate understanding of the people and events under investigation. The problem can be confounded when we are dealing with cultures and times that act in ways painful or foreign to our cultural perspective. Complex issues arise when myth, story, and history are all mixed up and we cannot tell one from the other. Most often, major mysteries arise from a complex combination of factors: some are based on errors in data collection and/ or large missing pieces; others are based on biases and value positions that are an integral part of every report and eyewitness account; and some are based on the overall goals and methods of the participants and their interpreters whether journalists, historians, social scientists, or government leaders. These kinds of questions raise issues of historical *construction* and whether we can ever arrive at a truthful and reliable accounting of a past event.

In some major mysteries too much evidence may be missing to be certain about anything. More often, even with excellent, reasonable interpretations of the data, too much is in dispute or the materials are heavily one-sided. Even with extensive knowledge and sound theory, the combination of missing information and deeply embedded values and emotions is so powerful that we cannot match accounts well enough to discern what happened with a high degree of probability. For these major mysteries we need to do a lot of digging (sometimes literally), to make careful step-by-step inferences, and to use a method of investigation that assists us in looking at events from viewpoints other than eyewitnesses and reporters—that is, independent of events or from a comparative stance. In effect, we attempt to sort out evidence by extrapolation, by inference, or through the application of explanatory theories designed to assist us in difficult situations.

Some mysteries in history are profound because the only way to satisfy ourselves with an explanation is by reading in from very limited evidence or by reading out by applying speculative or philosophical theories. Many discussions of early people, for instance, involve extrapolation from evidence or interpolation from theory, but so much is missing that we really cannot be sure about anything because there are no witnesses and no written accounts, not even a good dispute. All that is left may be a bunch of bones, a few tools, and some mysterious grave goods. So we do what we suspect people have always liked to do from the beginning of time, make up stories, put flesh on the bones, color in the dinosaur skeletons, giving them flesh and blood and even character. These may be more satisfying as literature, however, than as history, but only if you accept the notion that literature is less true than history (more about this later).

Furthermore, some major mysteries are very complex because they involve many parties with strong interests, passions, and viewpoints, who may not be willing or able to give an account that is anything but deeply flawed and full of bias. All such accounts are flawed, but we could counter this by corroboration with other accounts. However, there are occasions in history when "sidedness" gets out of hand and nearly all accounts available are partial, one-sided, mutually inconsistent, and/or disagree about facts, reasons, and values. This can leave us ready to throw up our hands in frustration because the mystery is a conundrum.

Perhaps the most in-depth historical mysteries are those that we see as evil—going against all social values, events that are inexplicable. Genocide, war, civil battles, and bloody rebellions often fall into the evils category, defying easy explanation even after an appeal for more evidence, better analysis, and philosophical evaluation. Where emotions run rampant and invade every pore and crevice of accounts, documents, past and present historians included, we are left with mysteries about human nature and human conduct. These debates, seemingly grounded on evidence and social theory, still result in extremely conflicted interpretations of events.

A major mystery often arises when human beings are so animated by events as to be unable to agree on almost anything worth using as a standard or criterion for compromise or consensus, particularly in a dispute. In this type of major mystery, even professional historians and social scientists fall prey to political influence, economic interests, or national fervor. You might call this, by current standards, a kind of Enron problem. Mysteries abound when people persist in viewing the evidence, themselves, their groups, their nations, their religions, their facts, their interpretations, their friends, their parents, their teams, their identifications, and emotional attachments as better than and superior to everyone else. The view is so superior that it justifies conquest, mayhem, torture, and degradation to achieve political or economic goals. Thus, there are plenty of major mysteries to discuss and debate with students, ranging from making sense of totally one-sided accounts of events, to philosophical debates about the meaning of human nature, to the uses of historical study. It could easily take a lifetime of detective work, teaching, and research to seek and find satisfying solutions to the great questions and mysteries of history.

# BE A DETECTIVE

As a test case, let us propose an historical problem to you and you decide what sort and what level of mystery is involved. We don't want to tell too much about this problem, but we admit that a bit of background and context does help, if it is available.[1]

* * *

Along a stretch of what is now southern Sweden at a place called Fossum, not too far from a major highway, is a ridge that geologists say was very close to the ocean shoreline several thousand years ago. Along this ridge is a stretch of exposed rock faces, not too high, perhaps between twenty and fifty feet up the side of the hill, covered with drawings that have been called *petroglyphs*—symbol writing or artwork. These were carved in the rock during a period known as the Bronze Age, before writing and before TV interviews, so it is impossible to find out what the people of that culture meant or had in mind when they did the rock carvings.

The great number of carvings in the same area and the repeated images imply that these were depictions perhaps of common events within the community, or perhaps fantasies about what the artists and/or community members would have liked to see happen. The very lack of clarity, the abundance of the drawings/carvings, and the exuberant (we say!) quality of the images stimulate questions and investigations—in short, detective work!

See Figure 1–1 for a small sample of the rock drawings of central near-coastal Bronze Age Sweden. Think about some of the questions here and add some of your own.

- What is your interpretation of the petroglyphs?
- How would you characterize their purpose and meaning?

---

[1]Based on Kaliff, Anders. n.d. *The Spirit of the Stone*. Tanum, Sweden: Vitlycke Museum Tanum Rock Art World Heritage Center.

FIG 1–1   Tanum: Rock carvings at Fossum (Sweden). Included on the World Heritage List of Protected sites.

- Why did the residents of the time place these images on stones for all to look at?

- Were they good artists, good historians for their time?

- What were the most deeply held values of the people of that time, as far as you can tell?

- How might such artifacts, such ruins, be used in a history classroom?

- What level of mystery is posed by these rock drawings?

- What complexity of mystery do you perceive in the evidence?

- Which kinds of related evidence would you like to have to bolster or revise your interpretations?

For your information, many artifacts, some skeletal remains, and lots of lovely Bronze Age implements were discovered in or near the vicinity of the rock drawings, but we are saving this for later, after you have thought about the quality of the mystery engendered by the bit of evidence provided here. The chapter Notes that follow list some tentative answers to these questions: What sort of things and/or products do you think the people who drew those pictures would leave behind? What kind of life did they lead? How much can you be certain about from their rock drawings? What can you probably only guess about? Why are you sometimes uncertain?

**NOTES**   The rock carvings, most in Bohuslan, Sweden, were carved during what is termed the Late Bronze Age, which lasted a long time, roughly from about 1500 to 500 or so before the Common Era, which ushered in the Iron Age. The Bronze Age as a whole is characterized by significant innovations in metal working (i.e., bronze casting and smithery) of great strength and often intricate artistry. These techniques swept most of Europe during the two-thousand-year period before the Christian era, and were found in widely different areas from Sweden to Ireland to Hungary to parts of Western Russia, indicating a common culture and lively trading patterns. Most characteristic of the Bronze Age products were the elaborate round axes, spearheads, fantastic horned helmets, drums, ceremonial shields, and wooden ships, a few of which have survived. Ships and shipbuilding played a central part in many people's lives during the Bronze Age since that was the fastest means of travel across great distances; and it was particularly central, apparently, to the groups who completed the rock carvings in Sweden.

Surprisingly, the ships' design was very much like Viking vessels that were used two thousand years later, implying cultural continuity. Many of the symbols carved in the rocks continue also, like sun shields, maypoles, and *cup* marks—imprints of cup bottoms containing a stick or a coin that has been inserted. Just what these mean is not entirely clear, but scholars believe that the symbols involved religious beliefs and customs focused on sun worship as a source of life, and perhaps a death cult as well, or perhaps both, with the inference that renewal would bring reincarnation. Many round discs have been discovered in Scandinavia, some carried in chariots, some on shields, while cup marks were carved or stamped widely, seemingly for luck or as offerings to nature spirits (elves or trolls) of popular belief. A major point is that because written records and interviews are not available, we must infer lifestyles and beliefs from mute carvings and artifacts, a process in which error is quite probable and conclusions are, at best, tentative.

**NOTE TO TEACHER**  These rock carvings, or petroglyphs, might be compared and contrasted with American archeological ruins such as those left behind by Vikings in North America and those drawn by Native American people in the Southwestern United States, particularly in New Mexico and Arizona.

**RESOURCES**
CLARK, J. G. D. 1977. *World Prehistory from a New Perspective*, 3rd. ed. Cambridge, UK: Cambridge University Press.
COLES, J. M., AND A. F. HARDING. 1979. *The Bronze Age in Europe*. London: Portland Press.

## Resources

APPLEBY, J., L. HUNT, AND M. JACOB. 1994. *Telling the Truth About History*. New York/London: Norton.
BRUNER, J. 1986. *Actual Minds, Possible Worlds*. Cambridge, MA: Harvard University Press.
DAVIES, N. Z. 1973. *The Return of Martin Guerre*. Cambridge, MA: Harvard University Press.
FERRO, M. 1984. *The Uses and Abuses of the Past: How History Is Taught*. London: Routledge.
HAND, LEARNED. 1952. *The Spirit of Liberty*. New York: Alfred A. Knopf, Inc.
HUSBANDS, CHRIS. 1996. *What Is History Teaching?: Language, Ideas, and Meaning in Learning About the Past*. Philadelphia: Open University Press.
LOWENTHAL, DAVID. 1985. *The Past Is a Foreign Country*. Cambridge, UK: Cambridge University Press.
WHITE, HAYDEN. 1973. *Metahistory*. Baltimore: Johns Hopkins University Press.

# 2 *Isn't History Always a Mystery?*
*Objectivity and Postmodernism, Plus Solving a Minor Mystery About the Vietnam War*

> In part it will be true, in part false; as a whole perhaps neither true nor false, but only the most convenient form of error. . . . The history written by historians . . . is thus a convenient blend of truth and fancy, of what we commonly distinguish as "fact" and "interpretation." . . . It should be a relief to us to renounce omniscience, to recognize that every generation, our own included, will, must inevitably, understand the past and anticipate the future in the light of its own restricted experience, must inevitably play on the dead whatever tricks it finds necessary for its own peace of mind.
> —CARL BECKER (1932, 229–30, 231, 235)

## Objectivity: What is it and is it achievable?

We are about to walk with you through a minor mystery and sketch out the medium and major mysteries beyond it. But first we want to have a broader conversation with you about facts because our understanding of them has much to do with the way we approach any case and build a mystery. Indeed, the evidence or facts determines much of our relationship to history.

Briefly, we are afraid that we are impaled (ouch!) on the horns of a dilemma, and one horn is the past. We believe it really happened. We also think that the past shaped our lives and is worth understanding. The other horn is the realization that the grand totality of all people's experiences, which we call *the past*, is unknowable because human memory is so fragile and self-centered. The contradiction between these perspectives on the past poses problems for history. We want to know the past that really happened (and we even try to do this for a living), but we do not think we can. Whether we lean toward one or the other, we must keep grasp of both horns, so the results can be upsetting and the conclusions temporary.

### Data, evidence, and issues

This brings us back to data, or *evidence* as we have been prone to call this basic stuff of history. Since the days of Otto Von Ranke, the dean of the historical profession at the time of the invention of the modern university in the 1880s in Germany, the attempt has been to recover facts from the past. When we get all the facts, according to Von Ranke, we will fit them into a narrative that re-creates and/or tells the story of the past (Novick 1988a). There are many problems with this idea, but let us start with facts.

What is a fact, evidence, or data? What did you have for lunch today? (We had pasta a la vodka from a pizza store on Broadway at 98th Street.) Whatever you answer is data. Now that we have written our answer down (even if it never makes it into the final manuscript and only stays as a draft on a hard drive), it is ever potentially available as part of the historical record. But will anyone care in a hundred years (even revising this a week later it seems trivial)? Some meals turn out to be more important than others. There are some people worrying about what President Zachary Taylor ate for dinner on July 4, 1849; he died of stomach pains a few days later, and there is some suspicion that he was poisoned. His dinner has been the subject of some discussion, and it matters; after all, he was the President of the United States (Parenti 1999).

There is more data out there than anyone can possibly record. We cannot even remember all the facts in our own lives; for example, do you remember what you ate for lunch two days ago, a week, a month, a year, or beyond? Wait! Maybe it was important after all. Your lunch might serve as a symbol or sign of cultural behavior; for example, there is a debate about how well-off artisans were in the colonial period. To try and settle that argument, historians have attempted to quantify the cost of 2,500 calories a day, and other scientists have tried to re-create from sources we can still find what artisans were eating. Or, maybe you are the child of immigrants and the way you blend food from your parents' traditions with other food eaten more regularly in America might have something to teach us about cultural patterns today. If you ordered your meal online, you could be an important part of the history of technology and everyday life in the twenty-first century. Perhaps you ate tuna fish that was caught with nets; future historians might lump your lunch in with other causes for the extinction of whales and dolphins. It is just not always clear what importance anyone will attach to any single item of evidence.

## Are historians creating evidence?

It seems quite possible that it is the historian, and not the evidence, that determines importance. Although you and your lunch really exist and are part of the past, the future historian determines whether, and how, they count in history. That meal matters if the historian writes about its value such as its ability to tell us about the economic well-being of artisans, or the assimilation of immigrants, or the President of the United States getting sick and dying shortly afterward. Much depends on who and what the historian or social scientist views as key to understanding the past.

In 1961, British historian E. H. Carr described this problem elegantly as the difference between a *mere fact*, one of an infinite number from the real past, and an *historical fact*. The historian, in Carr's words, "decides to which facts to give the floor, and in what order, or context" (Carr 1961, 9). So, if your lunch becomes important to one historian who writes one essay, it is a footnote to history. But if many historians are moved by the essay and quote it in their own work, the lunch becomes part of something very important; future students will have to learn about it and eventually it will show up on tests like the SAT II or AP exam. It will have become an historical fact. This process certainly depends more on historians than on the way the facts were experienced by those who lived them.

An example from oral history can help us explain how data, which may not have seemed important to the people who lived the events at the time, can become significant evidence a generation or two later. Historians conduct interviews with people who have something to tell them. Some labor history, for instance, can only be recovered by asking the striker on the scene about her or his views, since official records do not usually have the strikers' perspectives. But along with where people were standing, why they were striking, and who was in charge, the historian may ask about the role of women, whether workers, wives, or daughters in a mining strike. The interviewee might be a woman who worked in some capacity for a company or she might have been the wife, mother, or daughter of a worker, and she herself might not have thought about her role as a wife, mother, or daughter in the same way that we do today.

The historian is asking her to go back and impose present concerns on the past. She can do her best to tell the historian about what she thought at the time, about what she and other women did, and about how they were treated, and then see what people who hear that tape think. There were women at the time of the strike who may or may not have been workers, and they certainly played a role, so what they recall is *real* data. But the concept of a woman's role may not have been a part of people's thinking at the time; so while those roles existed in the past they are not simply *discovered*, they are partially created by the future. The historian takes the way she thinks in the present, and asks questions from the present about the past (Grele 1991).

Even the strikers who are giving the interviews think about the data differently now than they did at the time. It is possible to simply say that the way the people at the time experience an event is not necessarily the complete truth of the event, at least it doesn't seem so a generation or two later. Even if we had a time machine, people would still be observing and recording other people. Each observer has her or his own psychological perspective. For example, there are anthropologists who lived among natives and yet we are having a raging debate over the meaning and reliability of the analysis that results from their direct observation. Many suspect that the seminal fieldwork essays may say more about the anthropologists and their culture than they tell about the observed society's culture.

## Evidence, historians, and shaping the past

The study of American slavery provides a dramatic illustration of the power historians and their readers have to shape a past of their own based on what facts they glean from what happened. In 1918, Harvard University Press published a definitive book on slavery by Ulrich B. Phillips, a professor at the University of Michigan, then at Yale during the first half of the twentieth century. He taught his students *the fact* that the slaves were happy; he knew they were joyful, among other reasons, because of all of the happy songs they sang.

In the preface to his book, *American Negro Slavery*, he wrote that similar relationships existed in the army camp he was assigned to in Georgia (note the effects of personal experience and acculturation); he found that despite the superficial differences between being drafted rather than enslaved, and quartered in barracks not cabins, a "visitor to their company streets in evening hours enters nevertheless a plantation atmosphere." Phillips describes the following evening scene: "A hilarious party dashes in pursuit of a fugitive and gives him lashes with a belt moderately laid on." When questioned, the explanation is given that the victim is an "awnrooly nigger whose ways must be mended." The scene ends as "a throng" of "carefree Negroes" fill the air of the army camp with the "old time" song, "I ain' go' study war no mo'" (Phillips 1966, preface).

It seems clear to us that Ulrich Phillips found the chase hilarious, but the man who was beaten with a belt probably did not find it humorous, or think of himself as either "awnrooly" or in need of "mending." Instead, that man might have thought that his position as a soldier in the U.S. Army entitled him to some degree of respect. Ulrich Phillips interpreted that scene, as he read the evidence about the antebellum South, through a set of assumptions that today we find so flawed by racism that, despite all of the research and the many important insights contained in his books, they cannot give us a reliable account of the past.

Although by the fifties Harvard professors no longer taught that slaves were happy, they still assigned a textbook by historians Morrison and Commanger that, drawing on the work Phillips first published in 1918, considered the happiness of slaves a *fact* (Novick 1988a, 229). Textbook publishers reconsidered their views on slavery during the sixties after the Civil Rights Movement had achieved wide public notice. Now they understood slave songs quite differently. The songs had not changed, but the professors' and the nation's view had changed dramatically.

These examples of lunch, the role of women in a strike, and slaves' happiness explain why we are so nervous about using the term *fact*, and why we keep putting it in italics. The interpretation Phillips gave the slavery songs, in particular, shows why we prefer to use terms such as *evidence*, *data*, or *original sources*. The songs, as Phillips understood them, provided evidence for the happiness of African Americans during slavery; we would like to examine that evidence and question it. All evidence can be interpreted, questioned, and challenged. Interpretations can also be challenged. Facts, by definition, cannot be challenged in quite the same way because they have the ring of truth or at least are established. Once you have *the Truth*, there is no more need to ask questions. Since the goal of a mystery teaching strategy is to encourage questions, we suggest that you supply evidence and let the students sort through it and try to derive (or argue over) the *facts*. Over time, your students may prefer to use terms such as *data* themselves, and to talk about how their data or evidence supports their interpretations.

The story of American slavery as published by Harvard University Press and in many textbooks has another message for us beyond the power of the historian to create the *facts*. Most evidence or data that can be firmly enough established for us to call it a fact is quite dull and uninteresting. What you had for lunch the other day, the day the Constitution was ratified, your credit card number—these simple and easily established data probably do not mean much by themselves. The more interesting matters in history are not so easily dissolved into *facts*.

Take the question Phillips addressed and answered in part with the evidence provided by slavery songs. Were the slaves happy? That statement "the slaves were happy" sounds like a factual statement, but think about it for a second. It seems reasonable to say, "I was happy on Tuesday" and pass it off as a fact, but how can we be sure that a few days later you will not say "I thought I was happy last Tuesday but really, deep inside, I was miserable"? How can you know if the slaves were happy or sad? Or is that too broad a question? Being happy or sad is not the same kind of information as a date being Tuesday, July 4. A broad question is important to historians, but you cannot answer it with just a few dates, or even with just words from songs. The happiness or sadness of slaves is not really a *fact* at all, but a value judgment. Worse yet, it is a value judgment based on the human and very fallible grounds of emotion and prejudice.

Most of history consists of judgments, or values, and somehow in school these get passed off as *facts*. Most of the information that people would really like to know is about such big questions that evidence may not exist to answer the questions wholly or perfectly. You would think that it would be simple to figure out if America really was a land of opportunity—that is, did most immigrants experience upward social mobility in their lifetime? Instead, because it is difficult to track individuals over a decade in the nineteenth century, this is a hotly debated topic. Another question that sounds straightforward—Was home ownership a good economic strategy for workers, or would they have been better off renting homes and buying stocks?—also involves many assumptions and calculations using partial data and lots of guesses, and it presumes that workers could buy stocks. In another field, after two decades of serious debate we have no definitive answer as to whether slave labor was economically superior to free labor in the antebellum period, even though a host of useful issues have been raised by the debate. In short, a statement, such as "World War I started because of X," slips into a judgment based on all kinds of messy evidence, and deprives students of the chance to make their own judgments.

For all of the reasons just noted, we prefer that students encounter evidence, collect or derive their own facts, and ultimately argue about which interpretations are supported by what evidence in order to reach their own judgments. Viewing the past as mysterious and partially inaccessible, we want to pass on problems and ideas about solving them rather than present our interpretation, or anyone's flawed answers as unquestionable *fact*. From a teaching perspective, mysteriousness raises students' level of interest, and decision-making opportunities raise the degree and intensity of classroom participation.

## Postmodern views: For and against

Raising concerns about facts, evidence, and/or data makes the case for history as mystery and helps us promote the investigation of the language of evidence and judgment. But we also want to touch on some more recent historical narrative concerns, which are even more unsettling to our desire to believe that we can write confidently about the past. E. H. Carr, for one, raised his concern that the historian imposes order onto facts, but Hayden White, another historian, has charged that the facts in history are "as much imagined/invented as found" (1978, 600). On one level White is not saying anything much different from Carr—the past is formless and it is the historian who decides what about the past was significant. But White is saying much more than Carr about how we create, write, and re-create history.

## History, myth, and story—An uneasy relationship

In essence, White argues that there is no essential difference between history and literary fiction. "Neither the reality nor the meaning of history is 'out there' in the form of a story awaiting only the historian to discern its outline and identify the plot that comprises its meaning" (White 1978, 124). Like Carr and many others, White believes that there is no single correct view of any event, but many correct views. This does not mean that, anymore than Carr, White and others with the same view were implying that historians made up facts or were not in any way restricted by facts in their stories, but rather that *facts* are only a portion of making meaning.

A major goal of history is making meaning. "We can tell equally plausible, alternative, and even contradictory stories," White maintains, "without violating rules of evidence or critical standards" (1983, 136–37). White did not reject standards of evidence, he just found them less imposing when considering the "meaning of the past." Peter Novick, who wrote an award-winning book about debates over *objectivity* between American historians in the past century, has compared the work of historians to that of artists. A poet might face the constraints of a sonnet or a haiku, so many lines of so many syllables, and fail to produce a sonnet or a haiku on technical grounds. Within the form the poet can express any meaning.

So Novick argued that his own work followed no less (and no more) stringent rules regarding evidence, and he could "mine" the work of those whose interpretations he opposed for facts to support his arguments, but within those rules he could make any meaning he chose. In his words, "with minimal ingenuity you can construct a narrative of almost any imaginable shape, drawing whatever moral you wish, without getting the facts wrong" (Novick 1988b, 7). Novick advocated what he acknowledged was a utopian position, that historians stop making claims to truth and authority in their representations of the past. Instead, historians should admit "that what we are doing is exploring and thinking about the past with as much energy and intelligence as we can muster, and then making up interesting, provocative, even edifying stories about it as contributions to collective self-understandings" (Novick 1988b, 6). He insisted on factual accuracy, but argued that such accuracy does not truly limit interpretation and, for that reason, historians should give up claims to be writing something scientific and acknowledge that they produce works that are more artistic in nature.

White had a more specific notion of the limitations on historians and their ability to make meaning. This will not be entirely unfamiliar. Many of us are used to hearing all about the *story* in history. Usually someone is reminding us in our classes that we can make almost anything come alive, no matter how distant in time or space, when we share it with our students as a good story. But the concerns we want to discuss all take as a starting point the written quality of any history. Beyond focusing on the historian as an interpreter, as E. H. Carr did in pointing out the primacy of the historian over the facts, Hayden White points to the primacy of the writing over the historian.

Since we are writing a history-as-mystery book, we might as well make use of the analogy to detective stories. There are only so many ways to tell a story so that your readers can follow it and recognize it as part of the detective genre. There has to be some sort of crime, which we expect to resolve by the end. There are *whodunit* mysteries that search for the criminal, or motivation mysteries that know the killer all along but search for the reason needed to get a conviction. Agatha Christie wrote psychological thrillers, while Rex Stout's *Nero Wolfe* series was driven by the characters. Both authors started by setting the scene, adding a crime, then for most of the book following up suspects (more crimes might occur along the way) and ended with a revelation (if not a punishment) about the criminal. There are an infinite number of characters and plot twists possible, but all inside the basic format of the detective novel. The *Hardy Boys* or *Nancy Drew* series, whose adventures number in the hundreds, are rumored to have only five basic plots. If we do not like a detective novel, we are expressing a taste, making an aesthetic choice. If we think it was not just poorly written, but was a *bad* detective story, or was not *really* a detective story at all, we are saying that it violated conventions of the genre or that it followed the conventions only part of the time. We are not making a statement about *Truth* with a capital *T*, rather we are talking about our taste and our conventions.

History as story, as narrative, may allow the author as few choices about how to tell the story as any other genre, such as detective fiction. Hayden White calls history "a verbal structure in the form of a narrative prose discourse" (Novick 1988a, 600). In his analysis, most history is written in a meaning-making narrative (tells the story) using one of four literary *tropes*, or systems of making meaning. Using their Greek names, they are: metaphor, metonymy, synecdoche, and irony. Historians employ plot devices, according to White, much the same as a novelist by using romance, comedy, tragedy, or satire to foster comprehension and communicate values. White distinguished four modes of explanation and four ideological stances.

For our purposes, the specifics of White's exploration of historical writing (or any other scheme for that matter) matter far less than the central claim that historians as writers face limits no less (or more) significant than writers of mystery novels. There are only so many ways to tell the story, and the story controls meaning. (By the way, White does not, we think, mean those specific categories are eternal. Rather they are catalogs of what forms are available in our culture. Anything written in other forms will not be as comprehensible to us as history as the ones we are accustomed to reading or hearing.) While White's understanding still allows the rejection of work that violates certain technical rules, the main point—the interpretation offered by any history—can only be accepted or rejected on the same aesthetic or moral grounds one uses in preferring one detective writer over another.

---

### Be a Detective

In human beings, with their astonishing narrative gift, one of the principal forms of peacekeeping is their human gift for presenting, dramatizing, and explicating the mitigating circumstances surrounding conflict-threatening breaches in the ordinariness of life. The objective of such narrative is not to reconcile, not to legitimize, not even to excuse, but rather to explicate.

—JEROME BRUNER (1990, 95)

1. How can we interpret this quote by a modern psychologist, one interested in child development? What does Bruner mean when he says that narrative explicates or explains?

2. How does the human gift of narrative apply to history and history teaching? Would you ask your students to present, dramatize, and explicate the circumstances before a conflict? Would you give them enough time to work out their own interpretations?

3. Would Bruner agree with White that meaning and narrative go together? If narrative gives meaning, then are all stories equally good, equally useful, equally true in some sense? How can we tell story from evidence?

4. If storytelling is so powerful, then how can we draw students into the process of telling themselves rather than being told to? Any ideas?

---

## The big question: Why do history at all?

If history is only a *present* making of meaning out of traces of the past, why do it? If there is no past *out there* to confirm or deny the meaning we make out of the past, why not simply write fiction? Of course, many authors do. There have been several responses by historians who hold what are often called *postmodern* views. Hayden White believes that the stories we tell about the past can show us the randomness of existence. In other words, he claims that chance is a big factor in history, but people would prefer not to accept that as a meaning. And it is confrontation with the potential meaninglessness of the past that "alone can goad living human beings to make their lives different for themselves and their children, which is to say, to endow their lives with a meaning for which they alone are fully responsible" (White, cited in Jenkins 1995, 138). For many people, including some historians, meaninglessness is a source of terror, a void they try to fill. There are scholars, such as Beverly Southgate, who think it is possible to write history as a hypothesis about the past, not an absolute claim about the "past as it really was," in order to "change and create ourselves through the lessons we derive from the past, even as we acknowledge the lessons to be a creation of our own and our reading of the past, not absolutely inherent in the past" (Southgate 1996, 133).

For some, the answer has been that, having knocked objectivity off its throne, we can now go to the past in postmodern ways of doing history, whatever they might turn out to be, and write histories that help create our ideal futures; for Keith Jenkins that is life in "emancipated" human rights communities. Such a theoretical position is different from the ones advocated by Southgate and Novick who both want rules for the historical profession to follow, even if those rules do not result in absolute *Truth* about the past. Authors, such as Keith Jenkins, have suggested that without a discoverable past "out there" to refute anyone's writing, "there are no absolute grounds for determining what can and cannot be called 'history.'" He considered this problem an opportunity, not a tragedy.

In the early and mid-nineties when Jenkins wrote "Re-thinking History" and published an expanded version of the argument in *On "What Is History?"*, he believed that as new ways of writing history come into existence there can be more material available to help us become the sort of people who make a better world (1995, 42). But as Jenkins has continued to struggle with a history that has no *truth* basis for rules about what is and is not history, he has more recently suggested that we "do not need—and maybe never have needed—to measure our 'changes' against always highly selective images from the rear" (1999, 4). After grappling with these questions in print for well over a decade, Jenkins can only respond to "why bother with history" by answering that just as "stomachs do the kinds of things that stomachs do, and spleens just do the kinds of things that spleens do for reasons we cannot fully fathom, so human beings qua human beings just do seem to be of a kind that wants to find answers" in studying the past (1999, 5).

So, what do we think? Where are we, as teachers, faced with all of these problems? Should we really take postmodern criticism seriously when it claims that history is not much different from fiction, or history does no better than fiction in creating imaginary worlds that give us perspective on the present or on our lives? We have no final answers. What implications does this have for the kind of history we can teach on Monday? Briefly, in our practice, we are probably with Southgate and Novick, while as consumers of history, we stand with Jenkins or others who read the most skeptical and positioned parts of Hayden White as his most convincing arguments. We agree that, while there is a real past *out there*, it does not dictate what the historian writes. The past we teach *is* as much created as found. We create it in writing, through dramas, as films, and in our minds.

Although we teach a great deal about how to handle evidence and build hypotheses, and try to follow through when we write history, we suspect that Jenkins is possibly more on target when he claims that history is just another imaginary story than Southgate and Novick, who do not believe in objectivity but propose rules about honesty and correct facts they say can guide history and social science scholars. The discipline can erect rules, they say, and distinguish what is and is not history just as one can say whether something is a proper haiku or sonnet. This may get harder and harder to believe, and probably is harder to do in an age of docudramas, advertising, revisionism, and official sponsorship. Consider *Dutch*, the biography of Ronald Reagan by Edmund Morris, a reputable historian who inserted himself before he was even born (wow!) into a novelistic version of Reagan's life and calls it nonfiction (i.e., serious history). Although denounced by much of the historical community, the book was published and is out there, and it will get increasingly difficult to attack such popular sellers of human' images. Perhaps Morris is being more honest in explicitly writing himself in, since that is what historians do anyway when they write in dialog with their subject. Is this actually much different than history was in ancient times when the King or Queen authorized an official stele or stone commemorating his or her conquests and greatness?

No, we are a bit more complacent about the ability of history to "keep on keeping on" with more modest truth claims because of our version of Jenkins' "history-as-stomach/spleen" argument we mentioned earlier (if your eyes glazed over, go back and read it again). Although there may be no inherent reason why the past as it happened should affect the histories we write today, somehow it still does.

Although everyone has always (well, almost always) known that Jefferson was a slave owner, for example, the recent genetic tests suggesting that there is a high probability he (almost certainly?) slept with his slave Sally Hemings still rocked the country and the historical community. Most Jefferson scholars had once declared sleeping with Hemings incompatible with their understanding of Jefferson. Although no one forces them to say so, most do think differently of Jefferson now; some are even embarrassed. No one can force all historians to read the past the same way, and on some level, the reality of Jefferson as a slave owner should make the nature of his relationship with Sally Hemings irrelevant. But because we are human beings with feelings (or stomachs/spleens, if you will), it matters to us and it makes a difference.

This is an example of Justice Learned Hand's view (in the opening quotation of Chapter 1) that historical arguments erupt over and over, changing both the evidence and the way we see the evidence, bringing still more arguments about the past (and the present) in their wake. So, although perhaps these data should not have mattered, they did. The past that was *out there* played a role in reshaping our understanding of Jefferson. (We will explore this mystery further in Chapters 4 and 5—if you like, you can sneak a peek now.) This may be a cultural phenomenon and not an absolute characteristic of historical study, but nonetheless it helps us follow rules of evidence as writers while reinforcing our skepticism about interpretive claims as readers.

In this section, we have tried to address some pressing current concerns about the nature of history and facts. We have presented the postmodern view—the idea that history is suspect, subject to emotions, built on incomplete and biased evidence—perhaps, unknowable as truth, as proven fact. We have not done justice to any of these complicated arguments or problems. Those who are interested should follow-up by reading Novick, Jenkins, Southgate, and/or White. But we want to end with a final thought. In our experience, the histories that move people are not the bland textbook-style, fact-overstuffed, coverage-oriented lectures, blah, blah, blah. The histories that are talked about are the big, open-ended histories— the ones that raise questions and conjectures—in which there is room for mystery and the deeply mysterious.

# Teaching the Vietnam War as a mystery

So far in this book we have made a general case for why we see mystery in history and why we think teaching history as mystery makes sense. We also have set out some general principles for going about it. Now we would like to offer the Vietnam War as a concrete example of history as mystery. There are many good reasons to suggest Vietnam as a starting point, but one in particular moves us. Faced with the potential controversy teaching about Vietnam can provoke, textbooks and school systems have taken *neutral* approaches, and we have both experienced *boring* classes about the Vietnam War! So let's restore some mystery and challenge to this fascinating series of events that, paradoxically, so many of us care so much about yet usually can say very little of importance. Avoiding controversy may be good social manners on occasion, but in a classroom, it renders history as frozen and settled.

If you recall, we spoke of three levels of mystery: minor mysteries (solvable by the available evidence with a fair amount of certainty), medium mysteries (partially solvable at best), and major mysteries (very likely unsolvable with either evidence or theory). Aspects of the Vietnam War can work at all three levels, but in this example we concentrate on a minor mystery to start you off, and suggest some medium and major mysteries to explore later on. Keep in mind that we see these as a sliding scale of questions and solutions rather than as distinct divisions. The differences between minor, medium, and major mysteries are those of degree rather than kind. This concrete example should provide you, the reader, with a sense of what we, the authors, think of as a fairly easy, relatively quick mystery that is solvable by research (which we provide) and reasoning.

There are many mysteries to choose from concerning Vietnam, but from the perspective of U.S. involvement in a major shooting war, perhaps the clearest place to begin is the 1964 Gulf of Tonkin incident and the resolution that followed. Although our involvement, and the involvement of our French predecessors, with Vietnam dates to earlier times, this is the resolution that authorized the President to directly involve U.S. troops in offensive missions against North Vietnam. This resolution symbolizes the beginnings of open intervention in Vietnamese politics by the United States.

## A minor Vietnam mystery

What happened in the Gulf of Tonkin and how did it lead to the congressional resolution? Most textbooks dispense with the Gulf of Tonkin incident in about four sentences. Students learn the following:

- In early August 1964 North Vietnamese fired on one or two American ships in the Gulf of Tonkin.
- While there was some doubt about the attack taking place at the time, and now near certainty that there was no attack (remember the *Maine* whose sinking prompted the 1898 Spanish American War . . . even though it now seems

that it was not attacked), the Johnson administration used this moment to respond with force, directly attacking North Vietnam with American fire power.

- More significantly, the attack served as the trigger for the congressional Gulf of Tonkin Resolution that gave the President a *blank check*—the right to take "all necessary measures to repel any armed attack against the forces of the United States and to prevent further aggression."

- The resolution passed the House unanimously and only two Senators voted against it; shortly after this Johnson dramatically escalated U.S. involvement in the war.

These accurate and dry sentences display the weakness (in our view) of most history textbooks and some history teaching. In the rush to cover everything in an inoffensive way, teachers never let students work at any of the little mysteries that can be so much fun to tackle, and so satisfying to solve.

Let's take a moment to distinguish between learning more details about the event and creating a mystery. Although we both lean toward more depth and less broad coverage in our courses and teaching, it is not helpful, from a mystery perspective, to simply give your students all the *facts* of the case. Even though this basic account contains most of the relevant facts, it is no more mysterious than the briefer textbook version.

---

On August 2, 1964, an American destroyer was off the coast of Vietnam in the Gulf of Tonkin. Its mission was to provide covert electronic support to South Vietnamese raids on North Vietnam. The American ship encountered fire from North Vietnam. The Navy reported that the attack on the ship took place in international waters. The Navy sent a second ship as reinforcement. On August 4 that second ship reported that North Vietnamese PT boats had fired at it.

The National Security Council convened an immediate meeting. Secretary of Defense Robert McNamara reported that, while there was some confusion in the reports, there had been a significant naval engagement; and while there had been no American casualties, our ship had sunk two PT boats and fired on three to six.

After sending his initial report of an engagement, the commander of that second ship sent messages questioning it. The darkness and bad weather made him uncertain about what, if anything, had happened. Efforts to confirm the report from his ship, and from other military sources, failed. By the next day, the events of August 4 had become even more obscure.

---

This is the standard sketch of the event that you would find in any general account in a book dealing with Vietnam. We based this account on details provided in *The Wages of Globalism* (Brands 1994) and *A Bright and Shining Lie* (Sheehan 1988). You can certainly provoke debate in class about the response the United States should have taken on the basis of that limited information, or what kind of resolution Congress should have passed. That may be a useful lesson plan, but it is still not a mystery.

From our perspective, presenting students with the somewhat greater number of details in our handout does not, in and of itself, make the Gulf of Tonkin incident more mysterious or interesting than if students only heard the list of the four points we presented before. It is still a closed set of facts for students to remember. The problem is that teachers, textbook authors, and professional historians have worked too hard, and we have not asked students to work hard enough; and in the process, we are keeping all of the fun to ourselves.

Behind those dry factual narratives, of either four sentences or of four paragraphs, lies a pile of evidence. The items available range widely from the logs of the two ships, the *Maddox* and the *Turner Joy*, to transcripts of Defense Department hearings and congressional investigations, to the many interviews compiled by journalists and scholars over the years. Some of it is quite contradictory.

Here are twelve items—a Mystery Packet—that you can give your students to stimulate thinking about mystery, history, Vietnam, and problem solving in general.

# MYSTERY PACKET

The information here is a selection of data about an historical incident—the
Vietnam War's Gulf of Tonkin incident.

**ITEM ONE**   U.S. Navy Film

*VOICE-OVER as you see a re-creation of the scene*: In international waters in
the Gulf of Tonkin, destroyers of the U.S. Navy are assigned routine patrols from time to time. Sunday, August 2, 1964, the destroyer *Maddox*
was on such a partrol. Shortly after noon, the calm of the day is broken
as general quarters sounds. In a deliberate and unprovoked action, three
North Vietnam PT boats unleash a torpedo attack against the *Maddox*.
At once, the enemy patrol boats arc brought under fire by the destroyer.

**ITEM TWO**   Statement by U.S. Defense Secretary ROBERT MCNAMARA:

No, it [the *USS Maddox*] has no special relationship to any operations in that area
[North Vietnam]. We're carrying routine patrols of this kind on all over the world
all the time.

**ITEM THREE**   Next part of the U.S. Navy film:

Following the Sunday attack, the *Maddox* is joined by the *USS Turner Joy*. As
directed by the President of the United States, the *Maddox* and *Turner Joy*
resume patrol operations in the Gulf of Tonkin. On the night of August
4, North Vietnamese patrol boats strike again.

**ITEM FOUR**   Statement by GENERAL PHUNG THE TAI:

On the night of August 4, the United States made public that so-called "Gulf of
Tonkin incident." But the story was a fabrication, created by the U.S. National

Security Council. Even as the National Security Council met, American aircraft were being sent to destroy several areas of our country. In reality, the second Gulf of Tonkin incident never happened.

**ITEM FIVE** Information gleaned from *MADDOX* and *TURNER JOY* deck logs of August 2, 1964:

The *Maddox* noted that three enemy (North Vietnamese) vessels approached the ship. The attacks began at 5:08 P.M. Saigon time. At 5:34 P.M. Saigon time, four U.S. aircraft arrived on the scene. Maneuvering to close [to catch up] with the *Maddox*, the *USS Turner Joy* cruised toward the northwest at speeds of twenty-five knots beginning at 4:25 P.M. Saigon time. By 7:28 P.M. Saigon time, the *Turner Joy* sighted the *Maddox*; she was fifteen miles away. The *Turner Joy* sighted U.S. aircraft overhead at 7:44 P.M.

**ITEM SIX** Information gleaned from *Maddox* and *Turner Joy* deck logs and action reports of August 4, 1964:

The *Maddox*, traveling south out of the Gulf, met first three and then four "high-speed contacts," at 9:59 P.M. Saigon time. By 12:53 P.M. Saigon time, the *Maddox* was clear of the attackers according to its deck logs.
According to the *Turner Joy*'s action report, the attack began at 10:35 P.M. Saigon time. The deck logs report that enemy contacts had ceased and the attack was over by 1:22 A.M. Saigon time.

**ITEM SEVEN** Photographic evidence:

Photographic information does not exist for the 4 August attacks.

**ITEM EIGHT** Radar evidence:

The only strong radar contact made that night was at the time the *Maddox* fire-control radar locked on the *Turner Joy*.

**ITEM NINE** Visual/physical evidence:

No members of the crew visually sighted any enemy vessels. The ship reported no physical damage.

**ITEM TEN** Interrogation reports of captured North Vietnamese naval crewmen contained in the Seventh Fleet Exploitation Study:

Fuel, radar, and navigation limits kept the North Vietnamese navy squadrons operations area within 106.30ØE longitude.

**ITEM ELEVEN**   Official U.S. Navy history:

The 4 August incident occurred near 108.E longitude.

**ITEM TWELVE**   From naval records:

Leaving Keelung with a communications van on board, the *Maddox* was part of the Desoto Patrol program. Sent into the Tonkin Gulf to survey and gather intelligence from North Vietnam and China, the *Maddox* followed a predetermined schedule. The van, maintained by the Naval Security Group, contained electronic equipment used to gather and process Electronic Intelligence (ELINT). Designed to intercept communications and electronic emissions, the Desoto Patrol surveyed the coasts of North Vietnam and China. By emitting certain signals, the *Maddox* could make the North Vietnamese believe she was a force of ships or she could mask herself, deceiving them into thinking no ship was in the area. Along with the van, a contingent of trained personnel took station aboard the *Maddox*. Some personnel were from the Naval Security Group (NAVSECGRU) Taipei and some arrived for duty from NAVSECGRU Philippines. Those from the Phillippine were able to understand the Vietnamese language and those from Taipei could translate Chinese.

In the absence of a narrative, such as the one supplied by the textbook or the in-depth worksheet, students confronting the twelve items in the Mystery Packet must piece together their own account of the events in the Gulf of Tonkin. This is only a minor mystery, in our opinion, because the information already exists for students/readers to create their own, fairly reliable account of events. Rather than handing them a finished narrative, the puzzle challenges students to act as detectives and to put together the best account they can devise from the available evidence.

We want them to work from *evidence* rather than *facts*. The deck logs of the *USS Maddox* and the *USS Turner Joy* conflict on the times of the attacks, or the times when US planes flew overhead. What does this establish? It could mean that keeping accurate logs during combat is difficult, or a low priority. It could mean that these two ships had confused or distracted personnel. One ship could be accurate, or they both could be wrong. Students will have to figure out what deductions the evidence supports. There are other contradictions: Secretary of Defense Robert McNamara stated that the ship was on routine patrol. The history of the DeSoto Patrols suggests a different conclusion. What is the truth?[1]

We ourselves are not certain we can recite the facts of the incident, so we stick to the term *evidence*. Let the students argue over the facts they can derive from all of this material. Since nobody really knows with absolute certainty what happened in the Gulf of Tonkin on August 4, 1964, students can reach their own conclusions.

Solving this mystery requires relatively little historical context, though context certainly helps. The evidence is fairly self-contained; it needs to be played off against itself for contradictions. Our hope would be that a puzzle like this one will spark an interest in the students to look into other mysterious aspects of U.S. involvement in Vietnam. Minor mysteries can serve as springboards for medium and major mysteries—more important work, but more difficult.

## A medium Vietnam mystery: Was the war constitutional?

Did President Johnson, and later President Nixon, break the law and send tens of thousands of American soldiers and millions of Vietnamese soldiers and civilians to their deaths without proper authority? The U.S. Constitution grants Congress the power to "declare war" in Article I, section 8, clause 11. While the President is Commander-in-Chief of the Army and Navy (Article II), it is Congress that must raise, support, and provide for the governance of the Army and Navy; Congress must call up the militia; and Congress issues letters of marque and reprisal as well as makes rules for captures. No President ever sought, and no Congress ever passed, a Declaration of War on North Vietnam (or on North Korea, Grenada, Libya, Panama, not even on Iraq!). So, was the war unconstitutional?

---

[1]*Note*: If there was an attack, then the PT boat commanders knew that it happened, but if there was no attack after all, then even the North Vietnamese command must at least have wondered whether someone wandered into the path of the ships and fired without orders!?

We promised this would be brief, so here is the answer: maybe, possibly, probably not. There was a mutual assistance treaty that Congress had passed in 1954, there was the Gulf of Tonkin Resolution in 1964, and there were years of congressional appropriations and extensions of the draft. A few factors come in to play. Although Congress wants to protect its powers against Executive-branch encroachments, Senators and Representatives are often all too willing to let a war "belong" to the President, with all the attendant political risks, not ever taking a single declarative vote on a conflict. Other acts can reasonably stand in for an outright Declaration of War. The attack on Iraq in 1991 was preceded by a debate over the continuation of sanctions or the authorization of force. When an authorization of force carried, after debate over the use of ground forces, it sounded like a Declaration of War in all but name.

In the Vietnam case, the debate over the Gulf of Tonkin in the Senate on August 6 and 7 make for fascinating reading and provide all the evidence students need to investigate whether Congress thought it was passing the equivalent of a Declaration of War. For instance, Senator Morse quotes the Constitution and argues to the Senate that they *are* abdicating their responsibility and giving the President a *blank check* Declaration of War. Other Senators seek assurances that the President will not undertake a full-scare war without seeking additional authority. Senator Fullbright, sponsor of the legislation, both reassures them that the President has no such plan *and* refuses to state any specific limitation on the President. Senators do invoke the memory of Korea. There is plenty of evidence for either side, enough to support debate in class on whether the Gulf of Tonkin Resolution was a Declaration of War by other means. Later authorizations of people, money, and draft extensions can also be considered. The debate is published in the *Congressional Record*, so it is readily accessible.

What makes this a medium mystery? The ambiguity of what the Constitution might accept as legitimate congressional action tantamount to a Declaration of War moves this beyond the realm of a simple question that probably can be answered on the evidence. No matter what conclusions you reach about the record, there is an inescapable moment of interpretation when you also have to give your view of what is a constitutional war. In other words, *solving* these mysteries relies as much on your understanding of the question as it does your interpretation of the evidence. In a detective story, this is the distinction between understanding the evidence in the case and seeing what charge the law allows you to bring: murder, manslaughter, etc. We may agree on the evidence but disagree about whether it supports a charge of murder or a charge of manslaughter.

There are many other aspects of Vietnam that fit into this mold. Were the North Vietnamese and the South Vietnamese fighters communists, primarily, or nationalists/patriots? Was there (and at what times) enough cohesion to speak of South Vietnam as a country? Was attrition a legitimate military strategy? Did domestic opposition undermine military accomplishments? These are all questions on which some evidence can be gathered, but how your students choose to frame the question, or the standard they set for an answer—or the arguments they have over the *correct* understanding—will have much to do with the conclusions they reach.

## Major Vietnam mysteries

Some mysteries are in this category because the available evidence is so fragmentary we can never solve them, but that is not the case with Vietnam. So much about the war is in dispute that even with excellent, reasonable interpretations, extensive knowledge, and sound theory, values and emotions run so powerfully that we can't think clearly. We will just leave you with a few big questions that can frame these disputes in the classroom:

- Why was America involved in a war in Vietnam (was the Domino theory legitimate)?
- Why did America lose the war (could it have been won militarily, was the military simply held back)?
- Who benefited from the war?
- What does the war mean for America?
- What are the lessons of the war?

These are questions your students deserve to grapple with, and debate, and reach their own stalemates over. All too often, class is for presenting the facts while arriving at individual judgments or debating controversies is specifically avoided. There are *no* right answers—though there may well be many wrong answers, which isn't exactly the same—but the process of debating to find answers, of trying to solve the mystery, may be the most satisfying and engaging part of historical study. Students should experience it.

We will address the specifics of setting up a major mystery a little later on, but for the moment let us take a mental step backward and think about a progression from minor to medium to major Vietnam mysteries. These are not exact or additive. You cannot simply start with minor, go to medium, and end up at major. But maybe you can, sort of. Kids without much background can cut their teeth on the Gulf of Tonkin, and learn something about extracting deductions from evidence and trying to put a story together. If they follow that little mystery with the Senate debate over the Gulf of Tonkin Resolution, and attempt to interpret the "declare war" phrase in the Constitution, they are dealing with a significant degree of ambiguity. Now, there is a quantum leap between that ambiguity and the quagmire surrounding the question of *losing* Vietnam. Yet students who had examined a few medium mysteries (the nature of the North Vietnamese/South Vietnamese resistance, the steps toward U.S. involvement, My Lai, the idea of attrition) might be able to grasp the central ambiguity of the deep mysteries. They would not simply have to know that the debate was charged. They would also need to understand something about the nature of the mysterious relationship between the United States and Vietnam.

# Suggested activities: Teaching tips for the Gulf of Tonkin mystery

In coming chapters, we will spend more time discussing the creation and teaching of the mystery. Now, we just want to give you an idea of what we were thinking when we put the Gulf of Tonkin mystery together.

## Turning the Gulf of Tonkin back into a mystery

Creating this mystery took a bit more effort, though nothing too elaborate. We wish we had the actual deck logs, and more of the other original documents too. But the challenge we set was to see what material we could gather in under an hour of searching on the World Wide Web. Items one through four come from the transcript of "Lyndon Johnson Goes to War," one of the episodes of *Vietnam: A Television History* produced by PBS. The transcript is located on the local affiliate WGBH's website for their program, *The American Experience*. The information is pulled straight out of the transcription of the archival film they used in the program. Items five through twelve were pulled from a paper put online at Texas Tech University and accessed through a link from the Lyndon B. Johnson Presidential Library. Both are reputable sources and are consistent with the more general accounts available in standard history books. Since we grabbed the materials off the web, they were ready to arrange on the computer.

Making the event into a mystery required turning deductions back into evidence. The WGBH material was easy enough to use. It was simply a matter of removing the narration and letting the original material appear. The article took a bit more work. For example, the original presentation of the August 4 attack came with its own conclusion:

> The only strong radar contact made that night was at the time the *Maddox* fire-control radar locked on the *Turner Joy*. This is important in that enemy contacts, according to action report entrees, were reported to have passed between the *Maddox* and the *Turner Joy*. It is not clear how enemy ships, closer than the *Turner Joy*, could not be locked onto by radar.

We turned that into Item Eight, only reporting the lack of any other radar contact. The students will have to determine what deductions, if any, they can make from the evidence. We did much the same with similar information about the deck logs. Constructing this mystery did *not* require either elaborate knowledge of the Gulf of Tonkin, nor did it call for a home library on the Vietnam War.

Assembling the evidence also involved knowing what we wanted to leave out. One book, in recounting the attack, reports, "The American commander on the scene, noting the bad weather and darkness surrounding whatever had happened, began questioning his own reports almost as soon as he sent them, and subsequent confirmation efforts failed" (Brands 1994, 227). The twelve items we assembled generate considerable debate whenever we use them in a classroom. Adding an Item Thirteen, "the American commander on the scene sent a second telegram questioning whether an attack had ever occurred" would almost certainly close the debate, tipping it too far toward a clear conclusion that there was no August 4 attack. It would destroy the mystery. We are willing to withhold evidence or present partial documents in order to hand the class a mystery. We are willing to manufacture the mystery for the sake of the lesson.

## Classroom strategies

In the following sections, we apply the five suggestions we made about conducting mystery classes to teaching the Gulf of Tonkin mystery.

**A RULE IN FAVOR OF SHARED INQUIRY**   You need each student to investigate this evidence. Unlike some teaching situations where you need a student to give you the correct answer so that you can move on to the next point, the purpose of this exercise is to engage *every* student in making deductions. At a minimum, in a whole-class discussion reading the mystery together, you might simply go around in a round-robin asking each student how reliable they consider an item of evidence.

One teacher showed us a *tag-in* discussion method. You place five students in chairs at the front of the room and have them begin discussing the evidence. When someone in the "audience" disagrees or wants to further a point, he or she walks up to the front, "tags" one of the five students, sends the original speaker back into the audience, and takes his or her place and begins talking.

Participation is also encouraged by asking students to evaluate the material prior to whole-class discussions. We have had students individually read the materials at their desks and judge the reliability of the twelve items by rating each item on a scale of one (not reliable) to five (most reliable). If each student had to make comments about each item of evidence on a rating sheet that you collected, that would be another goad to ensure participation. Using small groups, we have asked students to share these ratings and to justify each one. We have had some groups reconstruct the chronology of the event; other groups simply answer the question, "What happened in the Gulf of Tonkin on August 4, 1964?" Following the individual or group work, it is much easier to gain participation from all students in a broader discussion.

**A RULE IN FAVOR OF *RAW* UNPOLISHED EVIDENCE AND DISAGREEMENTS AMONG WITNESSES**   This mystery contains direct disagreements such as the one between Secretary McNamara, the U.S. Navy film, and General Phung The Tai, and between the deck logs from the *Turner Joy* and the deck logs from the *Maddox*. There are indirect contradictions, as the history of the DeSoto Patrols conflicts with McNamara's assertion that it was a routine mission unrelated to Vietnam, or between naval intelligence reports on the range of North Vietnamese PT boats and the location of the attack.

These conflicting witnesses and types of evidence push students to consider the reliability of official statements from the Secretary of Defense or the U.S. Navy as well as the reliability of a general from North Vietnam. Is a film more or less reliable than a U.S. Navy ship deck log? What about the official U.S. Navy history of the DeSoto Patrols? Aren't all three items, the film, the log, and the official naval documents, history? Why might some be more or less reliable as sources about the event? If students have prerated the reliability of the evidence, this question may provoke a heated discussion, and if you are designing a sheet that your students will use to rate each item, you might have a column for the rating before the class discussion and a column for students to assign a new rating after the class discussion. These items are *raw* enough to allow a full consideration of contradiction and reliability.

**TEST EVIDENCE FOR TAMPERING AND REASONING FOR LOGIC**    Rating witnesses for reliability is one way of testing evidence, but there is far more to discuss with these partial items. Most of the items lack dates. When did General Phung The Tai make his statement? Would it matter if it was made in 1964 or in 1994? What was the context of McNamara's statement, a briefing to the President, a congressional hearing, or a press conference? How often are there contradictions in naval logs? What is the procedure for recording events? How reliable is naval intelligence or, more particularly, naval intelligence from Vietnam? There are many other questions to raise about partial evidence.

Still, there is room for rules. You can discuss the difference between proving a negative assertion and proving a positive assertion. It is difficult, often more difficult, to prove a negative statement that nothing happened. What might constitute a reasonable standard of proof for a nonevent? Can you develop rules that might prioritize the physical evidence from radar, photographs, and visual inspections for damage?

Another strategy for helping students explore alternatives is to reconstruct the event moment by moment, and make clear the decision points caused by what you deduce from the conflicting evidence. You can start with why the *Maddox* was in the Gulf in August at all. If you believe the navy film, it was a routine patrol; if you believe naval history, it was probably a more provocative surveillance or cover mission. If you believe that the *Maddox* was on a provocative mission, maybe that makes an attack more likely. So if the naval film is lying about the mission, it might even make Defense Secretary McNamara more credible!

Of course, just because the *USS Maddox* was on a more offensive mission does not mean that the forces of North Vietnam attacked. Even accepting that deduction, you can still tell both stories. You can work your way through the attack on August 2, 1964, toward August 4, 1964, 9:59 P.M. Saigon time, when one ship experienced an attack and one had not yet logged a contact. Going through the relatively short period of the attack, you can add in the different evidence and see how many different stories you can tell. If you have already rated the evidence as a class, you can decide which story seems to have the greatest amount of most reliable evidence supporting it, and the least amount of reliable evidence contradicting it.

**Play the questioner, devil's advocate, provacateur, innocent, ethical standard bearer—Ask, don't tell!**   Your role in the lesson is that of the coordinator, the board recorder, and the devil's advocate. As we have described this lesson, you drive it by suggesting activities such as rating the evidence, reconstructing the event, or exploring contradictions between witnesses. You need to push students to tell you if their deductions rule out possibilities, or if you can believe that the history of the DeSoto Patrols mean McNamara was lying about a routine patrol, but not necessarily about an attack. You can increase student participation by prediscussion activities, and by drawing out reluctant pupils. Just to keep them looking, you might even ask students if contradictions exist in the evidence where you do not see contradictions.

You do go beyond just a facilitator of the process by pushing them to make deductions from the evidence and by dealing with the quality of the individual items of evidence. You keep asking them to deal with more and more information. You push them to disagree with each other and then to clarify their disagreements. But, as much as possible, you make them add up the evidence and force each one of them, individually, to decide what happened in the Gulf of Tonkin, and then to articulate (maybe only in writing) why each person reached that conclusion. If this is the first mystery you are presenting, it is probably best that you do not tell them what you think happened (or failed to happen). By the end of the year, your students may be comfortable enough with their ability to analyze sources so that they will not be overly persuaded by your interpretation. And, if they want to know what most scholars think happened in the Gulf of Tonkin, they can always look it up.

**Use mystery to promote a sense of play, to energize a sense of accomplishment**
We hope that this extended discussion of how we have experienced and thought about teaching the Gulf of Tonkin minor mystery illustrates the relationship between conceptual work and a sense of play in your classroom. Students involved in reconstructing an event or rating evidence are doing the fun hard work that attracts historians to the profession. Debating in class over rules of evidence sharpens thinking skills while also giving different students the spotlight. And the mystery hanging over the evidence—What did happen in the Gulf of Tonkin?—drives the discussion. At its best, when students are passionately disagreeing about the reliability of the deck logs or the meaning of the radar records and what to conclude about the sequence of events, they have combined work and play. That combination, we hope, is what *history as mystery* is all about.

## Resources

Becker, Carl. 1932. "Everyman His Own Historian," 1931 Presidential address to the American Historical Association. *The American Historical Review* 37 (2): 221–36.

Brands, H. W. 1994. *The Wages of Globalism*. London: Oxford University Press.

BRUNER, JEROME. 1990. *Acts of Meaning*. Cambridge, MA: Harvard University Press.

CARR, E. H. 1961. *What Is History*. New York: Knopf.

ELY, JOHN. 1993. *War and Responsibility*. Princeton, NJ: Princeton University Press.

GRELE, RONALD. 1991. *Envelopes of Sound*, 2nd ed. New York: Praeger.

JENKINS, KEITH. 1995. *On "What Is History?"* London: Routledge.

JENKINS, KEITH. 1999. *Why History?* London: Routledge.

MORRIS, EDMUND. 1999. *Dutch: A Memoir of Ronald Reagan*. New York: Random House.

NOVICK, PETER. 1988a. *That Noble Dream: The "Objectivity Question" and the American Historical Profession*. London: Cambridge University Press.

NOVICK, PETER. 1988b. "(The Death of) The Ethics of Historical Practice (and Why I Am Not in Mourning)." *Annals of the American Academy of Political and Social Science* 560: 28–43.

PARENTI, MICHAEL. 1999. *History as Mystery*. San Francisco: City Lights Books.

PHILLIPS, ULRICH. 1969. *American Negro Slavery*. Baton Rouge, LA: Louisiana State University Press.

SHEEHAN, NEIL. 1988. *A Bright and Shining Lie*. New York: Vintage Books.

SOUTHGATE, BEVERLY. 1996. *History: What and Why?* London: Routledge.

WEITZMAN, KIM. 1996. "The Relevance of the Tonkin Gulf Incidents: U.S. Military Action in Vietnam, August, 1964." Paper delivered at the 1996 Vietnam Symposium at Texas Tech—After the Cold War: Reassessing Vietnam.

WHITE, HAYDEN. 1973. *Metahistory*. Baltimore: Johns Hopkins University Press.

WHITE, HAYDEN. 1978. *Tropics of Discourse: Essays in Cultural Criticism*. Baltimore: Johns Hopkins University Press, 124 (as cited by Novick in *That Noble Dream*, 600).

WHITE, HAYDEN. 1983. "The Politics of Historical Interpretation." In W.J.T. Mitchell, ed., *The Politics of Interpretation*, 136–37. Chicago (as cited by Novick in *That Noble Dream*, 602).

## WEBSITES

Vietnam: A Television History. LBJ Goes to War (1964–1965), Transcript at *www.pbs.org/wgbh/amex/Vietnam*. Click on the link for LBJ Goes to War.

Lyndon Johnson Library, Vietnam Index *www.lbjlib.utexas.edu*

The Texas Tech University Resources on Vietnam can be found at *www.vietnam.ttu.edu/vietnamcenter*

# 3

# Truer Than True
## Looking at Women in the Old West

[I]maginative truth . . . transcends what the historian can give you . . . history cannot come so near to human hearts and human passions as a good novel can. . . . To make a bygone age live again history must not merely be eked out by fiction, . . . it must be turned into a good novel.

—NATALIE ZEMON DAVIES (1987, 4–5)

How else can any past which by definition comprises events, processes, structures and so forth which are no longer perceivable, be represented . . . except in an imaginary way?

—HAYDEN WHITE (1987, 57)

## Introduction: Image and reality

This chapter focuses on the ways in which historical images form and are formed by myth and story, fiction and literature. Significant events, those which many agree are important to the story of a nation or people, may themselves be shaped and reshaped by later storywriters who capitalize on popular interests, images of which are so widely accepted that they actually replace reality. A mythic image can influence reality by changing the way we think, speak, write, and/or "paint" a picture of a person, or an event. In some cases, the events' players influence how they are seen by others for economic, social, and political purposes to the point at which individuals' *invented* selves replace their *historical* selves. On occasion, the individuals may forget who and what they were, in favor of their reconstructed images.

It is this gap between story and history that we investigate in this chapter. To do this, we focus on a somewhat neglected but fascinating area of study—women in the Old West. In general, women have been sadly neglected in American history, and particularly their part in the story of Western settlement. The whole period is usually seen as a *man's* time, when cowboys and Indians (also usually males) are breaking broncos, warring with one another, being brave, criminal, greedy, colorful, and legendary. Often, powerful images develop that we describe with words that are difficult to define. These are intangibles: a character described as having charisma, bravado, excitement, or a story with resonance, compelling drama, or power. Are there any women and women's stories from the Old West that fulfill these adjectives, any that are viewed as special, powerful, and accomplished?

Where are all the women in the story of the Old West? Neither *ordinary* women who came West with wagon trains and started farms with their husbands, nor women who were extraordinary like sharpshooters, performers, bandits, and the like are given much attention during this period of American history. Books and articles that were published during the Western craze of the 1960s and 1970s focus almost entirely on men and hardly mention women, except as supporting cast members.

The West and women, we believe, are especially productive for raising questions about the relationship between story and history, gender and visibility; we hold so many fanciful and probably stereotypical images of nineteenth-century moves Westward that the *Truth* may be a mystery. The Westward expansion in general has been mythologized to the point of absurdity in many cases, with cowboys, Indians, ranchers, sodbusters, gamblers, and all the rest of the cast squeezed into now commonly accepted styles and roles.

Women, in particular, both those who went West to work and settle and those who went West (or never went West) for adventure, have also been stereotyped. It is from this pool that we will draw images of famous and not-so-famous figures to raise questions about the mysterious ways in which history is converted into story. We can ask about what is left out and what is added in, and why. We can ask about the kinds of family values or business values or political policies each case or example represents. In sum, we can ask a lot of questions about how a story was formed and repeated, used and distributed to the general public who now believe it as a part of the *real* history of the Old West.

The role of popular literature and pictures in forming historical images is often overlooked and is a lovely mystery in the sense that, out of dozens of possibilities, only one or two become popular. Sometimes, those who become popular are *types* or characters (e.g., the women in the West who were *like* men and could ride, shoot, and fight), but for what reason:

- Is this because they are countercultural?
- Is this because many women and men sought models who were liberated in ways that the women they knew were not?
- Is this because the literary creation is so powerful?
- Is this because the characters are so true (or untrue) to life?
- Is this because our deeply held values and beliefs want to hear one story rather than another?
- Is this because the audience wants to be entertained rather than informed?
- Is this because of all of the above?

How images become part of the fabric of a culture is something of an evolving mystery, as participants cast and recast their views and aspirations.

As you can see, there is plenty to think about in relating story to history, and vice versa. As we engage case studies, literary examples, and biographies, we might well encounter medium and perhaps major mysteries that involve historiographical problems like the following:

- What kinds of sources are the images coming from and are these reliable?
- Were any errors made in transmitting images from the frontier to the city slickers?
- What gender biases crept into historical interpretations that were eventually transmitted as popular literature to the masses?
- Can we trust ourselves not to *pretty up* an historical person or to refrain from varnishing a good story just a bit more?

We encounter problems in which history is converted into stories that are easy to sell and promote business. Suddenly, history has economic goals, and the originals may suffer or be glorified in the process. We may encounter psychological theories, medium mysteries, that attempt to explain why one character, story, or model becomes dominant over many others and is widely accepted by most members of society while others are rejected or undervalued.

Most difficult of all, the stories and posters, programs and magazines of the time, up to the present, raise serious issues about just what and how we know history. Can we trust our data? Can we trust our scholars? Can we trust past contemporaries? Can we trust revisionist history seeking to correct past errors? In short, what and whom can we trust: this is a major mystery involving reliability, viewpoint, and issues requiring a great deal of work toward even a reasonably valid conclusion.

## Reconstructing the Past

Deciding on the relationship between history and story is a problem for which we need a bit of theory. We need to think about how the past is reproduced and portrayed on television and in the media, literature, film, texts, biographies, and autobiographies. Because we are human and have faulty memories, and because we also have interests and beliefs we hold dear, there is a tendency to rewrite and revise the past in ways that please us.

We argue that people like the past rewritten into a better story. We argue that people like the past reconstructed so that missing pieces are filled in to form a complete story, true or untrue, or partially true and partially untrue. We argue that people like the past revised to promote the sale of popular images and build affection for characters, whether real or stereotypes. We argue that people like to enjoy the past, particularly its resident characters, cleaned up and revamped so that the *moral* of the story is clear, enlightening, and satisfying, not ambiguous.

If you agree with this list of human needs for charm, satisfaction, catharsis, and ethical perfection, then you must also agree that many stories may very well be adaptations, inventions, or outright fabrications. So, we can use some ideas to deal with human entertainment needs while viewing images and reading narratives or literature, in this case about women in the Old West.

Many historians, most notably David Lowenthal in his book, *The Past Is a Foreign Country*, believe that we should approach any story in history with care and attention to how it is re-created and presented. He views the study of history as an act of re-creation, a project in restoration, a difficult journey trying to capture something that cannot ever be regained in its original state. After all, we are in the present and the past is gone and can never be regained unless, of course, we build a time machine and go "back to the future" (Lowenthal 1985). That works as a mythological film or story device but, alas, we don't have one we can jump into right now and use to visit the Wild West and join Annie Oakley when she toured with Buffalo Bill. We cannot decide for ourselves what the past was like—(although we, too, may not be perfect witnesses!); we must work through intermediaries: evidence, reconstructions, eyewitness accounts, objects, scholarly studies, and so on.

Loewenthal makes many suggestions for thinking about the past, and we can apply a few of his ideas to our present mystery. To bridge this gap, this mystery, between story and history, you might want to think about the past in terms of the following concepts and questions:

*Goals and motives*: What was the motive of an author in writing and promoting a particular story? Are there any clues to the author's motives? Are these commercial, social, moral, political, all of the above? Is a character or event neutral? Is there emulation of positive traits, disapproval of negatives? Are nationalist aims expressed/antichauvinist? How can we decide on the motives?

*Re-creations*: In checking history with stories, has the author or image-maker simply copied exactly what was available? Have they duplicated a story? Have they reproduced and reenacted? Have they filled in gaps, making an event or person whole? In short, how much is invention? How much based on evidence?

*Self-deception*: Are the eyewitnesses and reporters of the time clearly engaging in revising and dressing up the story, literally and figuratively, to make it more dramatic and appealing and admitting that it is so? Are they deceiving themselves (and you) into believing that these are true and accurate accounts of the past based on historical evidence that can be tested and checked against other records?

*Theatricality*: Are authors, image-makers, publicists, and others working to produce a satisfying and entertaining story using real ideals and models, positive and/or negative, and primary evidence from the past to heighten a sense of significance and vividness—a *you are there* feel?

*Moral compass:* Are the stories and histories balanced and fair in their treatment of gender, race, ethnic, and social class issues and values or are there indications of *reading in* or *reading back* our present values and beliefs into past times?

*Emulations/commemorations/chauvinism:* Are the stories and the histories alike or different in portraying characters and events in ways that promote nationalism, pride of country, success, and perhaps also demean or diminish the opposition, or lesser folk, in the story to a footnote, or to relegate them to a lesser or unimportant status?

Stories and histories can be subtly altered using words and images to promote a more positive or a more negative view of the past, and this seems to be particularly true of the Old West, which has a *cult* status in the United States and many other countries of the world. Much of the story of the West has been concocted to please the public, a public seeking entertainment and excitement rather than historical truth. In fact, one might say that there is a social demand for good media, a market demand for stories, drama, images, and music that people enjoy and may be willing to pay for in a theater or for their entertainment at home.

The Old West offers many, many possibilities in this area, as you might guess, and has been used, maybe overused, many times in our history. Even while the real events were taking place, the myths were being constructed by writers and publicists. Thus, as teachers, we have a golden opportunity to work with media mysteries, both in terms of the production and consumption of stories and histories, and in the comparison of sources and how they have been manipulated and shaped to meet the demands of a hungry public.

## Interpreting stories and images of past and present: Theory and application

Although women in the Old West serve as our case study for this chapter, we need some theory to assist our interpretation of what we are reading, viewing, and listening to about that era. Cowboys and Indians, cowgirls and horses, persist as attractive topics for historical narrative, display, dramatization, and entertainment up to and including the present; however, we don't always analyze what we are enjoying, or rejecting, or why we feel positively or negatively about an event or personality. So we need some big ideas to help us out in thinking about the Old West, and the female gender's portrayal during that time. We need to think about how history is converted to story and back again, and whether we lose or gain in the process, and from what point of view.

Since story and history are part of media, we offer you several concepts from media studies to use as guidelines for interpreting the past: policy, audience, market, and social demand. Research on media studies includes film, literature, music, history, documentary, art, and so on, in effect all representations promoted by individuals and corporations for public consumption. Each culture has rules and regulations for disseminating images and texts, sometimes set by the government (ours has rules against saying some words on TV and radio and distributing child pornography) and demands a certain sense of responsibility (e.g., you may not slander a person, make a false representation as truth, plagiarize, or present fiction as fact).

Media, however, tend to take liberties with *Truth* because they are in the business of serving a market that will pay for their services. The market often wants what is not accurate, true to history, or responsibly presented. The market may want sensational stuff, sordid stuff, superdramatic stuff! Thus, there is a built-in tension in society between responsible public policy and market demand, leaving the average person pushed and pulled simultaneously by commercial and legal, social and cultural forces. Some would argue that the media are situated "ideally, between the market and the state, between two forms of domination and control" (Raboy et al. 2001, 96). This tug-of-war between state and society has probably been true since the United States became a country but has, of course, become a lot more complex and problematical as the media have grown in power and influence, and society has become able to afford increasingly complex and costly forms of entertainment.

As noted before, there are four closely interrelated aspects of media studies that relate directly to historical problems and mysteries: policy, audience, market, and social demand. Each will, we hope, contribute to your overall understanding of, and ability to solve, the mysteries we present as Old West case studies of gender.

## *Policy: Public laws and governmental regulations*

Our society sets rules for communication and publicity, rules that have been agreed on after considerable argument and discussion among and between both consumers and producers of media. Advertising, copyright, censorship, audience ratings, and other measures of media use and influence are regulated to some degree by law, by government decree, and by social pressures. For example, the portrayal of sexual conduct or misconduct has changed markedly over the years, and the rules for its portrayal have also been altered to fit the state of politics and of the culture at the time. Yet there are also rules for freedom of speech and freedom of expression, which it is the government's job to uphold and enforce.

The Old West assuredly included many people who made a living by what we would view as immoral and illegal means (e.g., cattle rustling, horse thieving, prostitution, banditry, and so forth). Many of these characters were depicted positively at the time, others negatively, but the public policy of the time restricted, or tried to restrict, how these folks could be presented to the public. In some social circles, there was a preference for moral uplift in biographies, and an avoidance of unsavory characters or disturbing events, especially those enacted by the government itself through its army (e.g., the murder of Sitting Bull, Wounded Knee). In other circles, people desired exactly what others forbade.

In effect, what the laws and mores of the time seemed to be saying (and is it really any different now?) is that citizens, good citizens, ought to desire and demand what is socially acceptable, moral, just, and patriotic and to avoid the negative and the critical. Yet in terms of public policy in the United States, both then and now, there was and is a commitment to the ideals of free speech, press, and assembly, which, theoretically, assures the public of access to an accurate story and to public criticism of the media.

Public access and creative license, however, can combine to obscure or inflate historical persons to a point where *Truth* is lost in a sea of hype. At this point, we may have a medium or even a major mystery to solve just in sorting out the fanciful and invented from the real and the true, some of which may itself turn out to be a personal or a social invention. This is great fun for you and your students to research, but not easy to solve.

### You Decide

Several noted historians have been criticized for plagiarizing or inventing parts of their books on famous people. As public policy, where might you draw the line between story and history, and how do we tell the difference?

## Audience: Consumers and citizens

Audience may be viewed as all of the people *out there*, who are looking for a good story, entertainment, enjoyment, interest, and just plain fun. Audiences are complex and composed of many individuals, each of whom is a product of social status, education, gender relations, economic background, ethnicity and race, place, not simply consumers of media. Each has particular needs and interests, based on their backgrounds, culture and status, that impels (compels?) them to choose certain stories, certain histories, over others that they find less satisfying. Just why people choose one story over another is a profound mystery, particularly when that story may affect them deeply and alter their tastes. It is certainly not based simply on economics: witness the failure of many big-budget epic movies in the theaters and the success of many small-budget independent films.

The audience, in turn, may also alter the product the next time around since sales for one story will fall while sales for another will rise. However, the audience may not know what it wants until it sees or hears it; thus, the intersection between public policy, media, and audience is somewhat unpredictable. There are abundant examples of audience shifts in values and interests. For instance, the film *Dances with Wolves*, which depicts Native Americans as noble victims of government and popular oppression, would not have been conceivable a hundred years ago when there was little public sympathy for the plight of "Indians." The audience has changed and what they are interested in has been altered by history, media, and social change.

### You Decide

- When are audiences ready for a subject?
- How do advertisers decide on marketing a product, or a personality?
- Could films like *Malcolm X* have been made during the Civil Rights era, or could *Apocalypse Now* have been produced during the Vietnam War?

## Market: Supply and demand

The *market* may be viewed as those people who are looking for ways to enjoy themselves and have the money and time to invest in some form of literary, historical, musical, and/or artistic entertainment or as we now sometimes call it, *edutainment*—the intersection of education and entertainment. In history, edutainment and docudrama, and other conflations of genres, offer real problems in deciding what was real history and what was invented. Public policy, as expressed by government rules, stresses openness and freedom of access to media (e.g., the World Wide Web), as well as freedom of speech; however, the market has commercialized a large percentage of most stories and forms of entertainment. Even public broadcasting, public radio, and government publication services, which are supposed to hold to a stricter, more open standard of production and accuracy, have been subject to market pressures and financial issues, sometimes abandoning public productions in favor of market productions.

In a highly commercialized society, media are tempted to shape products to suit their audiences, but they often oversimplify their view of audience tastes and frequently overlook social and cultural sensitivities. In the past, when Buffalo Bill's Wild West Show was the hottest thing going and generated a huge demand for tickets, the audience was vitally important to his success. Bill was shrewd in aiming his show to public tastes, and took innovative steps to include real Indians (Sitting Bull) in his shows, as well as real and constructed Western women who could shoot, ride, and rope as well as or better than men. Annie Oakley, the girl sharpshooter, was one of his favorites; she was carefully crafted by herself and by Buffalo Bill's Show in advertisements, to appeal to the largely Eastern, urban audiences who attended performances.

### You Decide

- How many of you *out there* think that the Broadway musical show, *Annie Get Your Gun*, is an accurate historical portrayal of the Old West, of Annie Oakley, and of the other characters who surrounded her?
- How much of the show is invented to please an audience?
- How much is based on public policy? How much on market demand? How much on social responsibility? Get the score and the libretto and find out!

## Social demand

Social demand reflects the combination of private and public expectations about what constitutes the values, ideals, and critical assessment of media in all forms. You might say this is our *better* selves, our *ideal citizen* selves, operating in terms of what we would *like to see* produced and what we *hope to consume*. This is the mental space occupied by higher notions of justice, freedom, and mercy: demands for historical revision that gives a fair and balanced place in the story to race, gender, sexual orientation, handicap, and the disadvantaged. Social demand can exist as a lobby for overlooked heroines and heroes, it can work toward programming for responsible views of the environment, or it can prefer stereotypes and conformity. Social demand can also promote conservative religious and philosophical ideals, requesting that sexual content be restrained and kept in good taste; that violent topics and content be controlled by public policy, and that freedom of expression be limited in some forms that might shock, humiliate, or offend the public.

Therefore, social demand can work in both liberal or conservative channels for what is viewed as right, as beneficial to society, and as supportive of public policies that seem to benefit the majority of people while restricting media markets. Social demand interacts with public policy and markets and audiences, shaping both production and consumption to meet the perceived needs of the population, or part of it. As noted earlier in this chapter, we can think about the market and social demand in terms of motives, re-creations, self-deceptions, theatricality, moral compass, and commemoration or chauvinism. Which segment is happy with the story, the history, and the images demanded is a good question. The conflict and tensions between social and market demands often produces media no one wants to pay for or view or compromises that seem very dull indeed, both of which often are severely criticized for lacking entertainment or dramatic values.

How we see the Old West is a case in point, for both men and women, in that many of these characters, like us, were complex human beings with problems. Calamity Jane, our case study, was often criticized as a loose woman because she was apparently promiscuous to some extent. Just why, we are not sure, but many male readers undoubtedly found her story appealing and attractive and would have enjoyed escaping their narrow moral confines for an imagined Wild West full of engaging and inviting women sharpshooters. There is now, and was then, a social demand to suppress immoral and violent stories and to portray women, especially, as feminine ideals. Some who could also hold a male's role were considered very attractive because of their independence and free spirit, but this could be developed only up to a point in their media presentation, the point at which complaints would pour in or sales would drop off.

There was, and still is, a line beyond which the sexes can only move at their peril if they are to retain an attractive social and public image. Just how much independence a woman could display was open to question, but people would and did react when they felt the line was crossed. Just where that line is can be a mystery for us in examining the image of women (and men too) in the Old West.

There were many prominent Western women, some in show business, some in politics, and some involved in social causes, most of whom are probably unfamiliar to a lot of readers, largely because they never became media events and popular figures. Some, however, were selected for prominence by the press and publicists of the time who thought they would make appealing figures and boost book and Wild West show ticket sales. Many stories were ascribed to the few women who became icons of popular reading and imagination and are remembered to this day. Here we look at several images, stories, and histories of two of these women, Calamity Jane and Annie Oakley, who were celebrated in their day, and still live in American memory through musicals, films, history, and literature.

We analyze images, ask questions concerning documents, and investigate mysteries related to each of the two women, tying their representations to the overall image or picture we have of women in the Old West. There is room for a great deal of study about Calamity and Annie, in particular, and about Western women in general. This chapter provides you with only a taste of what is possible for you to work with and think about. For more details and in-depth analysis, you and your students should follow-up with expanded inquiries into literary, biographical, and historical sources of the times, as well as into scholarly studies about each historical figure. A list of possibilities to guide research, should you wish to create or to extend lessons about women in the Old West as part of American history, is your next piece of detective work.

---

### Be a Detective

Rent or buy two or three TV programs, Westerns, from the fifties or sixties, or seventies—*Gunsmoke, Have Gun, Will Travel, Ponderosa,* or *Dallas*—and watch them. Keep close track of the ways in which women are portrayed. If you want to be systematic, do a content analysis of a show or two, counting the number of women characters, the type of jobs women hold, and whether they are depicted positively or negatively.

Were any women shown in commanding roles, in important jobs, or were most farmers, homesteaders, or saloon keepers? How many were of the rootin', tootin', cowgirl variety? How many were equal to men?

---

## Annie and Calamity images and stories

Annie Oakley and Calamity Jane became two of the best-known women to represent the Old West to millions of people. Both have been depicted in films, stage shows, and musicals throughout the twentieth century. As of this writing, *Annie Get Your Gun*, a musical comedy based on Oakley's life, was playing on Broadway, and many of the tunes in it are familiar throughout this country and much of the world. The stories of both women typify many of the virtues and problems in portraying the Wild West, a favorite period of American history that has given birth to considerable song and story, publicity and theater.

### *Images*

In several studies of Annie Oakley and Calamity Jane, historians grapple with the mystery of their popularity, and the reasons why their stories, both true and fanciful versions, appeal to audiences of all ages. The public image of Annie Oakley, cowgirl sharpshooter, has probably received better treatment, and more positive treatment, than that of Calamity Jane. The media's efforts to portray each as a colorful Western woman was largely created in the late nineteenth and early twentieth centuries, greatly aided by the very popular Buffalo Bill's Wild West show, which toured much of the United States and Europe.

We hope that you will play historical detectives and carefully examine the selection of photographs, posters, and publications that portray both heroines here (see Figures 3–1 through 3–8). Compare the still photographs of Annie Oakley and Calamity Jane with the publicity posters and film portrayals of each woman. In particular, we ask you historical detectives to study the body language, style and dress, pose, and symbols in each picture (refer to Akeret 1973 for guidance). Which do you think were taken or offered for public consumption and which may have been private? Which pictures do you think are closest to the actual looks and personality of each woman, and how can we tell?

### Be a Detective

- How would you interpret each of the photographs of Calamity Jane, and Annie Oakley?
- Which images are most *realistic*, in your opinion? Which are least so, and why?
- Which are trying hardest to build a myth around each personality? How can you tell?
- Do you think the artist's drawing of Calamity Jane (Figure 3–2) got her *right* when compared to the photographs?
- Do you think the Hollywood character (Figure 3–4) *got it right* in portraying Annie Oakley?
- Do you think the nineteenth-century posters were faithful to each figure, or did they romanticize each person?
- In what ways do the fictional portrayals differ from, enhance, or diminish the image of each woman?
- Are there any elements of their story that are included or excluded from the publicity or the photographs?
- Do any imply or advertise their humble origins?
- Do any attest to their skill with guns?
- Which of the pictures were probably designed to enhance myth and legend?
- How can you decide?

Overall, would you say that Annie Oakley or Calamity Jane are better at managing the way their images are presented? Can any popular figure manage their image in the media? Do most of us, out here in the audience, prefer the mythic and legendary images or the more realistic and ordinary images of each woman's life? Why?

Create a few questions for students that will bring out the meaning of some aspect of each photograph and/or poster.

FIG 3–1   Annie Oakley in Brooklyn.

FIG 3–2 "Miss Annie Oakley, The Peerless Lady Wing-Shot" show poster for Buffalo Bill.

FIG 3–3    Annie Oakley in her first years with Buffalo Bill.

FIG 3–4   Annie Oakley.

FIG 3–5   "Only and Original Calamity Jane." Photo by L. A. Huffman, mid-1880s.

FIG 3–6   Publicity pose of Calamity Jane as a scout for General Crook.

FIG 3–7   Jean Arthur starred as Calamity Jane opposite Gary Cooper's Wild Bill Hickok in *The Plainsman* in 1936.

FIG 3–8   Calamity Jane line drawing captioned "Miss Martha Canary ('Calamity Jane') the female scout."

## Stories

You should share biographical information from an author or two with your students. Excerpts from the work of Isabelle Sayers, one of Annie Oakley's biographers, follow. We have taken the material here from a 1981 Dover edition, a paperback that might be inexpensive enough to allow you to provide a copy for each student in your class. This information can be studied as a factual account of Annie's life, but it could also be examined for the kind of rhetoric it presents about women who exemplify the Old West. For instance, you might ask if the account is generally neutral, or tends to picture Annie Oakley as a heroine and fighter.

You might direct students to think carefully about how their feelings are being influenced by the author, positively, negatively, both or neither by these excerpts from Sayers' book:

No more unlikely background for an internationally known markswoman could be imagined than that of Annie Oakley! Her parents, Jacob and Susan Moses, were Quakers who reared their children in a quiet, religious manner. Yet from this modest environment emerged one of the world's most famous entertainers. (1981, 1)

Mr. and Mrs. Moses settled on a small rented farm in northern Darke County, Ohio, and five more children were born. After Sarah Ellen came Phoebe Ann (Annie) on August 13, 1860, and later John and Hulda. One daughter died in infancy. (1981, 1)

Jacob died of pneumonia on February 11, 1866, leaving Susan with little but their lively family of seven. She tried to keep the home together by going into the community as a practical nurse, but jobs were scarce and the pay small. (1981, 1)

Several fathers and many problems later, Annie learned to shoot game to supplement the family income as a young woman, and tells the following story during a 1914 interview:

I managed to kill a great many ruffed grouse, quail and rabbits, all of which were quite plentiful in those days. My father [probably her stepfather, Joseph Shaw] was a mail carrier and made two trips a week to Greenville, which was the county seat, a distance of 20 or 40 miles a day. . . . On each trip, he carried my game, which he exchanged for ammunition, groceries, and necessities. (1981, 4)

Our biographer, Isabelle Sayers, goes on to tell us about Annie Oakley's modest sense of celebrity as she gained fame and fortune:

No one would be more surprised at the continuing popularity of biographical films and plays based on Annie Oakley's life than Bible-reading Annie herself. From the time she first assisted her husband in his act between scenes of a melodrama, she endured incredible hardships on the road. There were difficult bookings (which Butler took care of himself), the drafty trains and the miserable boardinghouses. Later, when she was famous and her life was more glamorous, it is still doubtful she ever thought her life would be romantically portrayed on stage and screen. (1981, 87)

Glenda Riley, writing about Annie Oakley's fame in a more recent essay, has a contrasting perspective you should share with students:

Oakley was not born in the West, nor did she make her home there. In fact, she traveled only occasionally in the West with Buffalo Bill's Wild West Exhibition. But in another way, Annie Oakley's story is crucial to understanding the American West. Oakley, who possessed an abundance of grit and grace, used these qualities to shape people's beliefs about the West. Through dazzling athletic skill, consummate show business acumen, and a captivating femininity, Oakley strongly influenced how Americans and Europeans viewed the American West—and in turn how Westerners often perceived themselves.

Between 1885 and 1902, the years when Oakley achieved fame with Buffalo Bill's Wild West as the peerless lady wing-shot, her interpretation of the West proved attractive to millions of people, at home and abroad, for she characterized the best of the West. She came from humble beginnings, maintained modesty throughout her meteoric career, and managed those mainstays of Western life—the horse and the gun—with exceptional skill. Oakley's West was one of straight shooting, fair play, and the triumph of good over evil. In addition, Oakley became the archetypal Western woman. As the person who created the genre "cowgirl," Annie projected an image so feminine, ladylike, Victorian, and beguiling that most people found themselves drawn to a woman who shot and rode horseback in public. Rather than being repelled by Annie's version of a strong, achieving woman, viewers cheered her onward and often came to believe that women—especially those of the Western variety—were fully capable of great feats and daring exploits. (Riley 1994, 93)

Is this passage just another variation on the same facts, or is this an interpretation of Oakley's life that is so different from what Sayers wrote that it might be about another person?

## The history and story of *Calamity Jane*

This chapter investigates several of the mysteries surrounding Calamity Jane. There are quite a variety of *unknowns* in Calamity's story, ranging from minor and medium to major mysteries. For example, you might involve students in what we consider a minor mystery concerning just how Calamity got her nickname. After all, she was born Martha Canary, not Calamity Jane, and came from very humble circumstances where celebrity nicknames were probably awarded to other people. You might point out that a lot of Western heroes and heroines had colorful nicknames, asking students to consider the reasons for such naming practices. Students can compare and contrast the five accounts of how Calamity received her nickname and discuss the historical problems of solving a simple naming mystery. How long after the events was Dora writing (see Document 2, p. 75)? How long after was Jane writing? Are either of these historically accurate and acceptable as *Truth* or are both self-serving?

In the stories and studies of Calamity, there is almost no agreement about how she got her nickname. One source alludes to noble reasons for her nickname involving Calamity's nursing of the ill and unfortunate, helping them to avoid calamity, while another source tells us that she was always bringing bad fortune to those she traveled with and that was the reason for the nickname. The various stories all seem quite different and agree only on the name and a few trivial details but not on the underlying story that gave Martha her new name. So, we have a minor mystery, a factual mystery, in which we can compare stories and take notes and study Calamity's autobiography and biographies to try to find out who has the best supported or most logical explanation about her nickname. Which stories and which reasons do you think were best and why?

We might also delve into Calamity Jane's story as a medium mystery of both self-deception and reconstruction through literature and history. The language of presentation of each of the accounts, autobiographical, biographical, and scholarly, are in stark contrast to each other and seem to be fulfilling different goals and motives for the authors. Perhaps you might like to ask students to read each of the five documents and decide if they think all five are pretty much alike in feel, tone, and style, or if they offer sharply contrasting pictures and moods about Calamity Jane. Why is it that when people write about themselves or other people, they work in such different styles and offer images that provide us with a wide variety of views and feelings about the characters? Why is it that historians and social scientists always try to write in more matter-of-fact tones and look for inconsistencies and hidden meanings in accounts?

Right off, Calamity's own account (Document 1, p. 74) seems poorly written and contains a lot of misspellings and bad grammar. She makes herself seem quite a gal who can ride and shoot and get along with men out on the wide-open range, and who is a heroine of sorts by helping out the U.S. Cavalry. Her explanation of how she got her name is rather fuzzy and the reasons cut short. Does that make her account more authentic sounding? Was Calamity really the author, or was there a ghostwriter who developed this based on some facts but mainly for sales in Deadwood?

Dora's account (Document 2) is better written than Calamity's reputed autobiography and makes her out to be a very colorful, if somewhat loose, character who was beloved but tough. In some ways, it agrees with Calamity's account but admits that it is based on tales of the old-timers who told these stories to Dora firsthand—but doesn't that make these secondhand accounts? Why does Dora (Madame) DuFran's account seem rather *mixed* in tone and portray Calamity as a rough-and-tumble woman who had a lot of problems, but could also be good-hearted? Is it any more objective than Calamity's story, or does Dora have a point she wants to make? Is she creating a theatrical perspective with a moral compass for Jane?

When we read Clairmonte's account (Document 3, p. 76) of Calamity's romance with Wild Bill Hickok, we really begin to wonder at the language used, which makes both of them sound heroic, tremendously attractive, and adventurous. The language glows with pride and is loaded with positive adjectives. It is a good read, and we might even want to get a copy and finish the entire life story, right now! Clairmonte has re-created a Calamity Jane with style and verve, someone we might want to emulate and be with on the range. There is also a new story about her nickname that does not agree with Jane's or Dora's. Just how does he involve us? What mystery of language and metaphor is he using to catch our interest and why? Does he tell us the real story or a story we want to hear, a story we demand from the market?

The scholar's accounts (Documents 4 and 5, p. 77, 78) seem rather mean-spirited and down-to-earth compared with the first three highly colorful and dramatic accounts. Their language is measured and critical, probing and questioning, and not particularly celebratory. Or maybe you don't agree? Do you? In any case, the scholars are quite critical of other people's accounts and suspicious about the degree and depth of invention or theatricality involved in the primary accounts. They are not very well-satisfied with the primary accounts themselves and accuse Calamity and her contemporaries of inventing yarns out of whole cloth, or at the very least partial cloth. In other words, the professional historians are less and less sure of what Calamity was really like and what truly happened than the stories of her time. Sollid (Document 4, p. 77) calls into question all of the tales about the nickname and ends on a note of uncertainty as to which story is most believable. Sollid goes into considerable detail in discussing Calamity's burial as Mrs. Burke, a family woman, rather than as the wild Western woman under her nickname; and as a good scholar, views controversies as theories to be cross-checked and tested.

The historian Etulain (Document 5, p. 78), in searching for accurate evidence of Calamity Jane's life in the Old West, expresses considerable dissatisfaction with most of the evidence available, arguing that the re-creations are predominantly theatrical or chauvinist and seek to convert a real human being into a stereotype of what people demand as a good story. Etulain also implies that most of the stories about Calamity were *stylized*, which might be a nice way of saying that we are reading literature, the *truth* of which is much like Hollywood movie versions of famous people—very far away! He seeks a plainer Jane, one closer to reality, a person who lived through considerable turmoil, personal tragedy, and tough times rather than a legendary female cowgirl. This historian wants us to see tragedy but also independence and gender issues, language very different from that used by the publicists of the time. Perhaps each account is rooted in its own time and its own theory about what is or is not important. In that case, we have a medium mystery and need to figure out how the manner of presentation changes our perception of history and historical figures.

In addition to the minor mystery of missing information, conflicting stories about nicknames, and the search for better and more reliable storytellers, we have added a medium mystery focused on the way language is used to convey history to us, the readers. We must face a mystery that raises questions about the use of facts and stories to create legends, and we have to try to separate tales from truth, although this is quite difficult to do in Calamity's case because these are so closely intertwined. Why story and metaphor are so important in Calamity's case can bring us from this little case study to a major mystery that concerns how we (and people's demands) re-create and reconstitute past people and events. In Calamity's case, a rather adventurous and self-reliant preteen from a poor and suffering family turns into a celebrity created by a media system hungry for good stories that fit a particular model, one that entertains without disturbing us too much, and one that portrays women as capable of independence but not enough to control their own destinies or stories.

A major mystery might center on the relationship between story and history, myth and accuracy, and whether it is possible to distinguish between the two in recounting and reconstructing the past. Perhaps the value system and beliefs of the time overpowered the true story of Calamity Jane to create a legend of the Old West that millions would find satisfying and enjoyable, avoiding the harder questions of frontier reality for women. Maybe current historical values and beliefs have propelled us to reconsider Calamity's story in light of gender and social issues that we were only barely conscious of earlier. This brings with it questions of class, race, sex, and social position that throw the life story of Martha Canary into a new and different light—does it? Do we always have major mysteries embedded in any story in the sense that we can raise questions about how knowledge is formed by historical methods and whether these methods can overcome, or at least neutralize, the market and social demands of the times in which we live? What do you think?

# CALAMITY JANE EXCERPTS

## DOCUMENT 1, C. 1896

My maiden name was Marthy Canary, was born in Princeton, Missouri. May 1st, 1852. Father and mother natives of Ohio. Had two brothers and three sisters, I being the oldest of the children. As a child, I always had a fondness for adventure and out-door exercise and especial fondness for horses which I began to ride at an early age and continued to do so until I became an expert rider being able to ride the most vicious and stubborn of horses, in fact the greater portion of my life in early times was spent in this manner.

In 1865 we emigrated from our home in Missouri by the overland route to Virginia City, Montana, taking five months to make the journey. While on the way the greater portion of my time was spent in hunting along with the men and hunters of the party, in fact I was at all times with the men when there was excitement and adventures to be had. By the time we reached Virginia City I was considered a remarkable good shot and a fearless rider for a girl of my age.

. . . Joined General Custer as a scout at Fort Russell, Wyoming, in 1870, and started for Arizona for the Indian Campaign. Up to this time I had always worn the costume of my sex. When I joined Custer I donned the uniform of a soldier. It was a bit awkward at first but I soon got to be perfectly at home in men's clothes.

Was in Arizona up to the winter of 1871 and during this time I had a great many adventures with the Indians, for as a scout I had a great many dangerous missions to perform and while I was in many close places always succeeded in getting away safely for by this time I was considered the most reckless and daring rider and one of the best shots in the western country . . . the campaign lasted until the fall of 1873.

It was during this campaign I was christened Calamity Jane. It was on Goose Creek, Wyoming, where the town of Sheridan is now located. Capt. Egan was in command of the Post. We were ordered to quell an uprising of the Indians, and were out for several days. When returning to the Post we were ambushed about a mile and a half from our destination. When fired upon Capt. Egan was shot. I was riding in advance and on hearing the firing turned in my saddle and saw the Captain reeling in his saddle. . . . I turned my horse and galloped back with all haste to his side and got there just in time to catch him as he was falling. I lifted him onto my horse in front of me and succeeded in getting him safely to the Fort. Capt. Egan on recovering, laughingly said: "I name you Calamity Jane, heroine of the plains": I have borne that name up to the present time.

—MARTHA CANARY (1969, 3)

## DOCUMENT 2, FIRSTHAND STORIES

Jane was reputed to be a sweetheart of Wild Bill Hickock. The men all liked her, being the only woman in camp. She had a good many womanly traits. She mended and washed for the men, cut their hair, and even tried to shave them, "But d—d near cut their throats," she confided later to a friend. This was her early life of the Wild West character known to us as, "Calamity Jane." As an old timer said: " Jane had a very affectionate nature." There were very few preachers around to bother her, so whenever she got tired of one man she soon selected a new one. But deeds, not morals, were needed in those days, and many can testify to the many good deeds she did. . . .

This woman of the Wild West, drank her whiskey straight, and plenty of it, swore like a blue streak, rode like an Indian, could shoot a bull's eye every shot, and yet gave the tenderest care to the sick or afflicted. At that time she was about the only woman in the tent towns of Lead and Deadwood, and did her duty to aid the sick in any way she could. Of course, when she was around they pulled a lot of good jokes, and Jane helped out.

She was often called "Mary Jane Canary," but this was nothing but a nickname. She liked to sing, but her voice was anything but musical, so they called her Canary after the mules, which were also called Rocky Mountain Canaries. . . .

In this story I have written only the tales I have heard from the early pioneers and her statements to me, personally. The people of today like to hear about doings of the old-timers in all parts of the United States; to seek out episodes of pioneers of the West. Calamity is one of the characters who has been given much notoriety and who has had reams of untrue stories written about her.

This ignorant, uneducated, untamed, unmoral, iron-hearted woman, who had been thrown among unfit associates from babyhood, played the part of a ministering angel in the life of the frontier. Ready to strip herself of the clothes on her back, if necessary, to do some poor soul a favor; buying a meal for some down-and-outer; paying a wash bill for some "unlucky" sister; easing the last moments of some poor miner hurt in a prospect hole; nursing men down with the smallpox, who would have died miserably all alone but for her gentle ministrations, for in those days smallpox was a very terrible menace in a mining camp far from civilization.

—DuFRAN (1932, 2–3)

## DOCUMENT 3, A ROMANTIC ACCOUNT

Near Laramie, Wyoming . . . it was there that Jane had a chance to see James Butler Hickok whose scouting record she knew about. When the men in the bar room suddenly went quiet, she followed their gaze toward the door, and Hickok entered . . .

Jane scarcely breathed while she looked at him, for she had never before seen anything that so well gratified her love of beauty. His soft full face colored with pleasure in response to the young men's deference, and his large chest heaved above a narrow waist and well-rounded hips. He had an aquiline nose and brown mustache that trailed, and his long chestnut-brown hair slightly wavy, was parted in the middle and flowing over its shoulders. His piercing blue-gray eyes looked over several heads and smiled at Jane, the only woman present.

He bowed at the waist like a Southern gentleman, and when he took a step toward her Jane noticed that he toed in. To her, this meant he was a true horseman . . .

She said to herself, "All this and the manners of a gentleman too!"

Among soldiers and ranchmen it was known that Hickok as a child had helped his father use his Illinois tavern, the Green Mountain House, as a station of the Underground Railroad. After his father's death, in his late teens he had come out West to make real for himself stories such as he had read about Kit Carson and Jim Bridger.

When he arrived he knew nobody in Leavenworth, Kansas Territory, but in a short time he was elected constable of Monticello Township . . .

She knew that since then he had guided General Sherman's troops across the plains, had been Deputy United States Marshal at Fort Riley to recover horses and mules stolen by deserters and rustlers, and that lately he had been scouting against the Indians.

No wonder she respected his record enough to hang back in the crowd. But he made a point of approaching her, and shook her hand. "I know who you are," he said graciously. "You're the Jane that's always on hand when somebody's sick or wounded. I figure you're always there for a calamity."

Jane was almost as tall as Wild Bill, and the two of them dwarfed most of the men standing around waiting for Frank Grouard to give them instructions.

"Tell you what," Wild Bill continued expansively, "I'm going to call you Calamity Jane, that's what! Say, fellows, how do you like that? I'm going to call Jane here Calamity Jane, because she's always ready to help out in a calamity."

A lightning flash of intuition seared Jane's solar plexus, and she knew that the name of Calamity Jane carried fame within itself. She saw herself as a character in history, and she vibrated with something deeper than vanity. Insight was traveling through her veins, prickling her arms and legs. She grinned, growing warm about the ears. She had sometimes envied Rowdy Kate and Lousy Liz and Pickhandle Nan for being popular enough to be given nicknames, but it hadn't occurred to her that such an honor might come her own way.

The men roared to show their approval of Wild Bill's suggestion—and it was because of this that Frank Grouard, on his record of the scouts he was that day engaging, added, "and Calamity Jane."

Jane was issued a uniform and rode off for Arizona at once

—Clairmonte (1959, 56–58)

## Document 4, historical perspective on the nickname

The origin of the nickname, Calamity Jane, has been dealt with by every old-time historian, journalist, mountebank and poor man's philosopher who has felt called upon to comment upon this woman of the frontier.

A few agree with George Hoshier, an old friend and pall-bearer at Calamity Jane's funeral, that she had the name early in life because she was prone to calamity. In the colorful words of that old pioneer, "if she sat on a fence rail it would rare up and buck her off." Another account states that she got the name after her outstanding service in Deadwood's smallpox epidemic of 1878 but by that time she had already been Calamity Jane for several years. The *St. Paul Dispatch* of July 13, 1901, explained it as follows:

> "She gets her name from a faculty she has had of producing a ruction at any time and place and on short notice." Dr. V. T. McGillycuddy stated that she was called Calamity because of the calamitous deaths of her father and mother. Since the topographer has been shown to be a writer of doubtful reliability, this theory can also be questioned.

Perhaps the earliest and most imaginative account of the captious appellation appeared in a highly fictionalized story, "Calamity Jane, Queen of the Plains." In that sensational tale, Jesse James inquired about her doleful sobriquet. Her gloomy reply to that frontier bad man is as follows:

> When I went to a mining town in Colorada at first, I was simply known as Jane—by some called "Pretty Jane." But wherever I went some great evil came upon some of the men or their families. . . . Their wives would fall into old shafts and break their necks, some of the men would accidentally shoot themselves, or so it was supposed, when a man was found with a barrel of his own pistol empty and he dead beside it on the ground. Children belonging to such men got lost, and weren't found till they had starved to death in some lone gulch. And as wherever I moved these things happened, people began to think I had the "evil eye" and carried bad luck with me, and they called me Calamity Jane. I've borne the ominous name for years.

In addition to scores of suggestions like the ones mentioned, there are two main versions, each of which has numerous adherents. The first theory appeared in Calamity's Autobiography, which was not published till 1896. Calamity may have been giving the same thrilling story long before that to a generation of "bar-flies" and "greenhorns." She may just once have been cajoled by the hoax-lovers into reenacting the scene for a crowd of "tenderfeet," and been stuck with the story. Estelline Bennett's uncle, General Dawson, stated once that Calamity Jane in her later days had lost track of which stories were true and which were not. . . .

The first contemporary mention of her as Calamity Jane was February 21, 1876, when I. N. Bard wrote in his diary: "Calamity Jane is here going up with the troops." The *Laramie Boomerang* was founded in 1881, at least five years after she became Calamity. Bill Nye came from Wisconsin to Wyoming in the late Spring of 1876 and began his Western newspaper career on the *Laramie Daily Sentinel* sometime after May 10. Three months previously, Mr. Bard saw Martha Cannary whome he referred to as Calamity Jane. It is, however, possible that the great humorist, Nye, did at one time suggest that Calamity Jane was so named because "hard luck and Martha Cannary always went hand in hand," but under no circumstance could he have done the original naming in either the *Sentinel* or the *Boomerang*.

Perhaps Martha Canary was not named Calamity Jane because of any one particular episode such as the Goose Creek incident or by any person as respected as Bill Nye. In the early days even the most casual observer of that lewd "Jane-about-town" must have noticed that activity seemed to spring up where ever she was, and conversely, that she followed excitement wherever it went. So, it is possible that Martha could have become Calamity Jane by the slightest accident.

Calamity Jane never did say that any part of her real name included "Jane." In the first sentence of her Autobiography she stated: "My maiden name was Martha Cannary. . . ." When she was buried in Deadwood her tombstone was marked Mrs. M. E. Burke. Her husband's name was Clinton Burke so there was no confusion of initials between Calamity and Mr. Burke. Since Jane, the second work of the nickname, was so important in Calamity's career, why did she not mention her maiden name as Martha Jane Cannary? Deadwood residents knew her as Calamity Jane for years and yet they buried her not M. J. but M. E. Burke. The answer might be that Jane was not her middle name and that whatever her middle name was, it began with an *E*. Today, especially in society on Calamity's level, a young woman is often called a skirt, a twist, a femme, or by an old expression, a Jane. That latter title might well have been used by many in the middle 1870s when referring to Calamity. How easy for someone talking about the escapades of Martha E. Cannary to have said: "Calamity sure follows Jane and I guess from all I hear that Jane follows calamity. Maybe we ought to call her Calamity Jane." From some such statement the epithet could have taken hold and stuck. In an age of Madame Moustache, Kitty the Schemer, Deadwood Dick, and Wild Bill Hickok, a name like Calamity Jane would have had no trouble immediately becoming part of the frontier vocabulary.

—SOLLID (1958, 33–39)

## DOCUMENT 5, AN INDEPENDENT WOMAN

When Martha Canary came riding with Wild Bill Hickok into booming Deadwood, South Dakota, in midsummer 1876, she was already known in the northern West as Calamity Jane. Just barely out of her teens, Calamity was gaining a reputation through sensational newspaper accounts as a young woman without moorings, rumored to drink and cohabit with abandon. In the decade and a half after that memorable summer in Deadwood,

Calamity was frequently dubbed a "hellcat in red britches," a Lady Wildcat, and a female terror of the plains and became a favorite subject for journalistic hyperbole. But behind this adventuresome, gun-toting hellion was another person: Martha Canary, a young woman adrift in a pioneer man's world, without home, family, or occupation. When Martha was transformed into Calamity Jane, her less-dramatic side disappeared under a landslide of purple prose. The pioneer young woman of the frontier lost out to the Wild Woman of the West. Behind the mythological figure of popular attire stands another woman who needs [to have] her story told. . . .

Unfortunately, in the more than ninety years since Calamity's death, no one has uncovered much of her past. Since Calamity was probably illiterate, there are no signed records—not even a signature. But there [are] an overabundance of lively stories: Calamity came to town, went on a wild toot, and is currently in the cooler. The paucity of solid facts and the plethora of stylized stories force Calamity's biographer to sort through thousands of bits and fragments to stitch together a story, much of it at odds with most of her previous life stories. . . .

Even before she became a teenager, Martha was without parents or a home. Unstable and uncertain as it was, life with Robert and Charlotte [her parents] had given her a semblance of home. Now even that was gone [with their untimely deaths]. What would she do? How could she find a home and provide food and clothing for herself and her younger siblings? . . .

Years later, Calamity's nephew, Tobe Borner, provided a few details about his aunt's next few years. When he pressed his mother, Lana, Calamity's younger sister, for the story of her early years, she told him that Calamity once blurted out defensively that she had turned to prostitution to provide for her sister and brother, Elijah (Lije). On another occasion, Tobe mentioned that the children were farmed out to Mormon families in Salt Lake City, but that Martha soon struck out on her own. One must remember that Martha was only eleven in 1867. . . .

If Martha Canary disappeared in 1870, she reappeared as Calamity Jane in 1875–76. In five or six years, Martha lost her identity as a wayward young orphan dependent on sympathetic adults for all her needs, but she was reborn Calamity Jane: an independent, devil-may-care young woman of alarming and antisocial antics whose reputation was known throughout the bordering Rocky Mountain and Plains states. . . .

Unable to remain rooted in one place, wobbling through a series of "marriages" and "husbands," and increasingly exhibiting abnormal behavior and mounting alcoholism, Calamity tumbled downward even as her magic name was recognized in widening circles. Two promising opportunities to act out her life and reputation in dramatic shows also collapsed because of her inebriate actions. The youthful, animal-like energy that sustained her through years of dissipation, instability, and drunkenness now betrayed her. At her death at age forty-seven, she was already a tired, sick, old woman.

But Calamity was more than a Wild West heroine, more than simply "one of the boys," more than a tragic figure. She was also an independent woman trying to find her way in an American West rapidly closing out its frontier years.

—Etulain (1997, 77–79)

# Suggested activities: Teaching about myths, fiction, and literature

There is a long-standing relationship between history and literature, language and perception of the past. Often, portrayals of people, places, and events seem more *real* in literature and the media than they do in the actual documents and sources from which we learn about history. A good writer can make an historical account seem far more glamorous and exciting, or less so, than the actual event. In some instances, popular figures, such as Annie Oakley and Calamity Jane, generate their own literature which may overwhelm the real-life stories of such women. The same holds true for any events, personalities, or times that hold romantic appeal for an audience, or for which an audience feels deep and abiding nostalgia.

In America, the Old West, the Wild West, the Frontier, all have a special meaning and evoke images of cowboys and Indians, cowgirls and horses, gamblers and marshals, conflicts between ranchers and sodbusters—in short, a whole host of images and attitudes that we often take for granted. These images also have meaning for the present and have been updated and kept alive through films, Westerns, musicals, operas, and literature. On careful investigation, however, many parts of these stories may have been invented for a variety of reasons: literary, economic, political, and social. We probably prefer Western heroines who are of middle- or upper-class origin, who may act like men in some ways but don't challenge men. We like adventure and prefer heroines who have had many positive adventures and wonderful skills such as sharpshooting and horsepersonship. If the real women are not up to our expectations, then we clean them up so that they look a good deal better than they actually were in life. We now have so many media for presentation—media that can improve almost any story or image we feed in, and for almost any purpose.

Therefore, we may use literature to develop a series of mysteries with our students. Some are minor mysteries about collecting and checking accurate sources; others are medium mysteries about how literary myths and legends are born out of much more prosaic materials. Major mysteries are about the process of historical inquiry itself in a situation where facts and evidence are absorbed and altered by myths and fiction that seems truer to the original than the original was to itself.

Mysteries present themselves when images and stories are compared, and we are faced with the problem of sorting stories from corroborated evidence, and *manufactured* and publicity images from natural, unposed, images. This is no easy task; it requires considerable comprehension of the images and identification of errors and purposeful falsification from varying viewpoints. A medium mystery to be sure! Just analyzing and comparing the viewpoints of people, photographers, literary journalists, and biographers ought to fascinate any student of history in your classroom.

To assist you in promoting a sense of mystery surrounding mythic figures, we have used two women of the Old West as case studies, but you can decide to pursue many more activities using the ideas we provided here and those that follow.

1. Collect photographs of cowboys as well as Western women and compare these pictures with the stage and screen images of cowboy and cowgirl actors and actresses. There are plenty of possibilities for comparison: Wild Bill Hickok, Wyatt Earp, the James brothers, Annie Oakley, Calamity Jane, Belle Starr, and so on. Or choose a character of your own from another time.

2. Contrast male and female singers of the Old West (early recordings are available from the Smithsonian and other collections) with more recent Country and Western numbers on the same topics, or even reinterpretations of the same songs.

3. Read biographies of Buffalo Bill and Sitting Bull and find out what happened to each one of them in life: Who got rich? Who became famous? Who lived to a ripe old age? Who was ambushed by soldiers? Share these biographies with students (excerpts are fine) and discover if your (and their) images of Sitting Bull and Buffalo Bill match the facts. Can you solve the mysteries of their images: Were they true to life or constructed to satisfy audiences, or both, or neither?

4. Lead a discussion about why some stories are so pleasing and have become the basis for musical comedies, theater, and such, while other stories have been ignored or avoided. Do any *risky* stories generate films, literature, or legends? Would Geronimo qualify as risky?—after all, he was a rebel and left an autobiography but has also been the subject of several Hollywood films. Were the films respectful of Chief Geronimo's own account or not? Why do writers like to make up their own versions?

5. Discuss how and why stories are invented. Ask students to create a story, preferably a Western, about someone they know. Who would they choose for the role of hero or heroine, who for villain or scoundrel, and who for Indian Chief? Can they make the story *realistic* and avoid stereotypes, myths, and fictions, or is that nearly impossible? Why?

6. Ask if social and market demands operate right now in our lives. Which stories are popular on TV and in films or theater now? Why have Westerns nearly died out? Why doesn't the frontier seem to hold the same romantic appeal for an audience? What type of heroines have the greatest appeal for an audience and how can you measure it? Does appeal change with changing times? Were Western heroines different in the 1880s, 1920s, and 1980s? Now? Should we check audience ratings for each network or for certain programs? Will that solve our mystery, or are human yearnings more complicated than that?

7. Take a shot at reconstructing the past and ask, What *sold* then? What was popular and what was not? Would you be willing to spend time and money wandering a Wild West town and take part in a gunfight, rustle horses, or watch cowboys (usually not cowgirls) lasso broncos? What would you find believable as opposed to mythologically pleasing about a Wild West show, a ghosttown in the West, a rodeo, a Country and Western dance complete with boots, bows, fiddles, and gals wearing gingham?

8. Study a book on historiography and learn more about the ways in which professional historians of the West, or of any era, try to separate fact from fiction, myth from reality. Save excerpts from two or three historians in which they discuss the ease or difficulty with which they distinguished myth from history. If you want to get into a good argument, read some of the latest revisions of Biblical history, or of Cold War history, or of the Israeli/Palestinian conflict.

9. Dig into at least two or three biographies of a famous figure, male or female, who helped settle or unsettle the West, purposely choosing authors from different time periods. Compare their treatments of the subject, as well as how the historians portray them, their mood, language, evaluation, or *moral compass*, if you will. Can judgments be avoided? Do comparisons lead to corroboration of the evidence or to wider disagreements? Are there any methods that could help us to reach consensus on a person, place, and/or event in the past, one that would help us to faithfully re-create the Old West?

10. Ask a series of questions about the materials presented in this chapter. Ask about the images and perceptions women's and men's lives in the Old West your students held before reading this chapter and whether these have changed. Ask about why we hold certain images and stereotypes of characters and types in the Old West and where these came from—past facts or suggestions from later fiction. Ask about the ways in which we can distinguish between myth and reality when we attempt to capture a past time in American history and literature. Ask the following and/or other questions of your own invention:

    - Why have certain people been turned into myths while others have not?
    - Why do we like to fill in missing data with drama and colorful details rather than admit to a lack of knowledge?
    - Why have particular personalities been turned into cult figures while others have faded?
    - Why does literature do a much better job (usually) of holding our memories and attention than history and social science reports?
    - Why do people need and want stories to believe in that may not be, and probably are not, faithful to history?
    - What are the motives behind the stories and myths about the past?
    - When do people become nostalgic about the past and try to *recapture* it?
    - How are images controlled by the media and to what purpose?
    - Why do some *stories* last, like Annie Oakley's and Calamity Jane's, while others disappear?
    - Have you ever sought out a story that has dropped out of popular lore and read it?
    - How are people changed as they enter the *mainstream* of history?

- Why are some people changed into *theatrical* characters while others are not?
- Who do we emulate and honor, and who do we vilify and hate?
- Is there any pattern to our likes and dislikes, any social demand for re-creations, for particular times and places, people and events?
- How do historians try to correct or contribute to literary and media images?
- Why are images, stereotypes, and publicity creations believed for long periods of time and then fall prey to debunking, revision, and criticism?
- Do images and stories direct us to *moral* lessons?
- Do authors have a *moral compass* that drives them, or is it just simply gain and lucre that matter?

## Conclusion: Creating myths and legends about women in the Old West

How and why we convert history into myth and legend, or vice versa, is a fascinating topic that you can use time and again with your classes when studying a wide range of topics in American and world history. Mysteries abound on the topic of comparing myths, legends, and literature with historical documentation. Minor detective problems deal with searches to fill out and check incomplete and/or reconstructed data about people, places, and events, such as our two Wild West examples—Calamity Jane and Annie Oakley.

Medium mysteries might focus on the subtexts, or underlying motives, for the style and evolution of language and images used to describe and portray people and places, especially popular figures who have been the subject of stories, films, and dramas. The reliability of the images, their pose, composition, meaning, and message, inadvertent errors and purposeful propaganda, may be part of a medium mystery in which we try to understand the way publicity shaped our view of the Old West and its women.

These medium mysteries might slide into major mysteries that call on teachers and classroom detectives to compare and contrast media presentations, tall tales, and publicity with the actual, down-to-earth accounts of famous people who often started out as *just plain folks*. This investigation process might be called, "Will the real Calamity Jane please stand up!"; here we try to separate all of the fanciful and largely invented stories—all of which, remember, have a reason and motive for their existence, to please social and market demands—from their more "homely" basis in historical evidence.

With minor, medium, and major mysteries, we ought to call attention to the ways in which historians go about investigating materials, sorting out the more believable from the less believable, and constructing interpretations and criticisms by adhering to standards for corroboration and consistency within and between eyewitnesses and reporters. A big problem with myth and literature is that the fictional accounts, often based on fact, may be likely to sweep us away with their power, striking images, and beautiful or colorful language. If we don't know any better, and avoid conducting any research, or suspend judgment, then the movie or story images capture our conception of another time and place, blotting out reality. In some cases, as in Calamity's, the myths and legends of a struggling, tough, but rather poor woman who liked to drink, take on a life of their own because they are so much more fun than the real thing. In addition, because there is often a fine line between entertainment and history, we want to accept the colorful and fantastic as *the* story, avoiding difficult problems of accuracy and any implications that our heroine might have had financial, social, and/or gender problems.

In the case of Annie Oakley, who was also from humble origins and had a tough early life, with perhaps a good deal more initial guidance and social development than Calamity, we find someone who at least somewhat successfully managed her own image as fame and fortune grew. Annie was a highly skilled sharpshooter (and a woman, no less!) but seems also to have been lucky and strong-minded. She married Frank Butler, an experienced showman and entrepreneur, and was in a successful and long-lasting union that worked to the benefit of both as they became part of the most famous Wild West show in America under the direction of Buffalo Bill Cody. Even Annie, however, could not control the process of popularization and mythmaking as she became a favorite subject of many dramas, musicals, and stories, each tending to exaggerate, embellish, and idealize her accomplishments.

Finding the real Annie Oakley (symbol of the Wild West, but an Ohio girl) and the real Calamity Jane (a real Westerner, but less of a symbol) takes a lot of detective work. As we sort out and read fantastical stories about each, it is also a good deal of fun and gives us a good sense of how an historian operates when dissecting and reconstructing popular fiction. We also wonder why some people and their stories become symbols of the West, or India, or World War I, or Native Americans: Why do their stories appeal so much to an audience while others do not?

In this chapter, we have presented suggestions for several mysteries you can try to solve with your students using the Wild West and two famous women as cases in point for mythmaking in history. The evidence and questions we provide here should be viewed as an appetizer for a full-scale inquiry, particularly aimed at the confluence of myth and history, image and reality. These contents are only a foretaste of what an historian or social scientist needs to accomplish for a better and more insightful understanding of the past, and the people who lived in it. You, as the teacher, can experiment with the ideas and examples we have given you, and you can change them, adding new materials of your own, switching to different subjects, and extending into new areas.

As we write this, new mysteries appear before our eyes every day, some very dramatic ones that we can't help thinking about because we both live in New York and have family in Washington, DC. This is, of course, the attack on the World

Trade Center and Pentagon. In this case, the reality may be more horrifying than the media presentations, but we are still faced with obtaining knowledge about this event through the media. We are never quite sure what is being included or excluded from discussions, nor can we control our need for high drama and storytelling. Worse yet, this is a complex major mystery, at least right now, because we don't know precisely who the attackers were, where they all came from, or what their true motives were in carrying out the attacks. A catastrophic event took place and we are largely at the bottom of a news funnel for which we have little perspective and less objectivity. How easy it is to study Calamity Jane and Annie Oakley by comparison with the World Trade Center attack! Yet the smallest examples and the greatest ones share a sense of the unknown and the undiscovered that fascinates us, raises disturbing questions, and demands investigation, solution, conclusion. We want answers!

## Resources

ADAMS, D. 1958. *The Gentle Tamers: Women of the Old Wild West*. New York: Putnam.

AIKMAN, D. 1927. *Calamity Jane and the Lady Wildcats*. New York: Henry Holt and Company.

AKERET, R. 1973. *Photoanalysis: How to Interpret the Hidden Psychological Meaning of Personal and Public Photographs*. New York: Pocket Books.

ALLMENDINGER, B. 1998. *The Ten Most Wanted: The New Western Literature*. New York/London: Routledge.

ARMITAGE, S. 1994. "Women and the New Western History." In Organization of American Historians, *Magazine of History* 9(1): 22–28.

CLAIRMONTE, G. 1959. *Calamity Was Her Name*. Denver, CO: Sage Books.

CODY, W. F. 1920. *Buffalo Bill's Life Story: An Autobiography*. New York: Holt, Rinehart.

DAVIES, N. Z. 1987. *Fiction in the Archives*. Oxford: Polity Press.

DuFRAN DORA (D. Dee) (brothel madam). 1932. *Low Down on Calamity Jane*. Deadwood, SD: Helen Rezzato.

EASTON, J. 1941. *Narcissa Whitman: Pioneer of Oregon*. New York: Harcourt, Brace.

ETULAIN, R., G. Riley, and R. ETULAIN, eds. 1997. "Calamity Jane: Independent Woman of the Wild West." In *By Grit and Grace: Eleven Women Who Shaped the American West*, 93–115. Golden, CO: Fulcrum Publishing.

GROSSMAN, J. R., ed. 1994. *The Frontier in American Culture: Essays by Richard White and Patricia Nelson Limerick*. Chicago: An Exhibition at the Newberry Library, published in conjunction with Berkeley: University of California Press.

HARMAN, S. W. 1954. *Belle Starr: The Female Desperado*. Houston: Frontier Press of Texas.

HAVIGHURST, W. 1954. *Annie Oakley of the Wild West*. New York: Macmillan.

JOHNSON, D. M. 1965. *Some Went West*. New York: Dodd, Mead.

JORDAN, T. 1982. *Cowgirls: Women of the American West*. Garden City, NY: Anchor.

KASPAR, S. 1992. *Annie Oakley*. Norman: University of Oklahoma Press.

LEVIN, E. 1989. *Ready, Aim, Fire!: The Real Adventures of Annie Oakley*. New York: Scholastic.

LIMERICK, PATRICIA NELSON. 1987. *The Legacy of Conquest: The Unbroken Past of the American West*. New York/London: W. W. Norton.

LOWENTHAL, D. 1985. *The Past Is a Foreign Country*. Cambridge/New York: Cambridge University Press.

MASTUMOTO, V. J., AND B. ALLMENDINGER, eds. 1999. *Over the Edge: Remapping the American West*. Berkeley: University of California Press.

OAKLEY, A. 1914. *Powders I Have Used*. Wilmington, DE: DuPont Powder Company.

RABOY, M., ET AL. 2001. "Media Policy, Audiences, and Social Demand." In *Television and New Media* 2(2): 95–115. Thousand Oaks, CA: Sage Periodical Publications.

RILEY, G. 1994. *The Life and Legacy of Annie Oakley*. Norman: University of Oklahoma Press.

SAYERS, I. S. 1981. *Annie Oakley's and Buffalo Bill's Wild West*. New York: Dover Publications.

SOLLID, R. B. 1958. *Calamity Jane: A Study in Historical Criticism*. Helena, MT: Western Press/Historical Society of Montana.

STEVENSON, E. 1994. *Figures in a Western Landscape*. Baltimore: Johns Hopkins University Press.

TOLL, R. C. 1976. *On with the Show: The First Century of Show Business in America*. New York: Oxford University Press.

WEIZMAN, D. 1976. *Underfoot: An Everyday Guide to Exploring the American Past*. New York: Charles Scribner's Sons.

WEST, ELLIOT. 1994. "Families in the West." In Organization of American Historians, *Magazine of History* 9(1): 18–22.

WHITE, H. 1978. *Tropics of Discourse*. Baltimore: Johns Hopkins University Press.

WHITE, H. 1987. *The Content of the Form*. Baltimore: Johns Hopkins University Press.

# 4

## Solved Mysteries?
### The Case of Thomas Jefferson and Sally Hemings

Although paternity cannot be established with absolute certainty, our evaluation of the best evidence available suggests the strong likelihood that Thomas Jefferson and Sally Hemings had a relationship over time that led to the birth of one, and perhaps all, of the known children of Sally Hemings. We recognize that honorable people can disagree on this subject, as indeed they have for over two hundred years. Further, we know that the historical record has gaps that perhaps can never be filled and mysteries that can never be fully resolved. Finally, we stand ready to review any fresh evidence at any time and to reassess our understanding of the matter in light of more complete information.

—Daniel P. Jordan, Ph.D., President,
Thomas Jefferson Memorial Foundation, Inc. (January 26, 2000)

## Introduction: Solved Mysteries

We have argued that presenting students with mysteries and evidence produces more involved and intellectually challenging classes than teaching history through *canned* explanations and lists of *facts*. We have also pressed the point that a mystery approach is more faithful to the way historians proceed, and more truthful, since we often do not really know *the Truth* about the past. In Chapter 2, we presented a case that is still a mystery, the events in the Gulf of Tonkin in August 1964. In this chapter, we explore what use we can make of mysteries when new information sheds light on an old story and causes our generation to reexamine thinking about a specific part of the past.

Here we consider what classroom use we can make of mysteries even when they are apparently solved. Even though no answer to an historical controversy is likely to be 100 percent certain, new technologies such as DNA testing, or newly released sources, such as the KGB archives of the former Soviet Union, can provide evidence that seems to tip the scales from ambiguity closer toward certainty. What difference does an answer to a long-standing mystery make in our understanding of history? What does it change? How much do mysteries matter? How do we teach about them once they are no longer mysteries?

The impetus for this chapter on the lives of Jefferson and Hemings originally came from the revelations about Alger Hiss and the Rosenbergs that followed from the opening of KGB archives. According to the current readings of the evidence, Alger Hiss did spy for the Soviets, and the Rosenbergs did pass on atomic secrets. They were all guilty of some espionage but resolving the mysteries did not resolve the debates around their cases. There are still debates about the significance of the information that they did pass along, of how much damage they did. Beyond the specifics of their cases, some writers have argued that, although there were still excesses committed, McCarthy was right to start a "Red" hunt—there were spies and traitors throughout the government. Counterarguments concede that some of the highest-profile cases were made against traitors, but emphasize that the records reveal no more than about 150 Americans spying in any significant way. This hardly seems like enough to justify any of the broad charges of treason in the state department, or among ordinary Americans, raised during the fifties.

As we were thinking about writing this book, the Sally Hemings/Thomas Jefferson DNA testing story broke in November 1998. The story reappeared in January 2000 with the news that the Thomas Jefferson Foundation, Inc. (then named the Thomas Jefferson Memorial Foundation) had accepted the findings and would make them a part of the interpretation at Monticello, the third President's Virginia estate. The solution to a two-hundred-year-old mystery, although not everyone involved has conceded that the study proves Jefferson's paternity of Hemings' children, prompted rounds of furious debates. Some concern contemporary race relations, raising issues about what this new revelation about Jefferson and Hemings tells us about ourselves.

Finally, the 2000 election controversy broke at the end of the semester, and at one point during our writing, daily reports were being issued from Florida over the postelection vote counts. Some showed George W. Bush winning even with recounts, others showed Al Gore the victor if all the balloting machines had worked properly. With all of the recounts now conducted by various accounting and media groups, data is available to treat the 2000 election as a *solved* mystery. We can date one draft of this chapter by ex-Senator Bob Kerrey's war crimes story (*New York Times*, April 29, 2001), and the new unsolved mystery that has come into being over what happened one night in Thanh Phong, Vietnam. When that new question will be resolved, or as to which other historical mysteries are ripe for solution, we do not propose to speculate at this time. Who knows what the future of the past will be?

Seeing the Jefferson and Hemings affair on the front page of *The New York Times* helped us realize that historical solutions do not just *turn up*. Someone has to be looking for the evidence that will resolve them, and others have to cooperate in supplying it or allowing the search. To hold someone's attention, these mysteries have to have meaning of one kind or another, and for them to get the play that lets us hear about solutions means that they resonate in our present culture. In the midst of all of these historical mysteries jumping off the front pages of the newspapers, generating lots of scholarly books and journal articles, we understood something useful for teaching about the past using solved mysteries. *Solved* mysteries are likely to be just those mysteries that have high-stakes and charged meanings for us today; otherwise, why would someone bother to reexamine them?

The controversy around the Jefferson/Hemings relationship lends itself nicely to a mystery approach. Beyond the question of whether they had a sexual relationship, we can ask further questions. First, what does the answer to the long-standing mystery of their relationship mean for us? A second stimulating question is: What difference does it make? How do we understand that important past event, and therefore ourselves, differently? Pursuing these questions helps us and students realize that our understanding of the past molds our ideas about the world *and* that our present worldview also shapes our understanding of the past.

The locus of inquiry in history is "the complex relationship between the past and the present." When students grasp this point about themselves, they can apply the idea of an interaction between past and present to examining the writing of several generations of historians and explore another derivative question: How have historians looked at the mystery all the years that it was seen as unsolved? Why did the historians think Jefferson and Hemings might have had a sexual relationship or might not have had a sexual relationship? Even when the original event in the past is solved, the way the past itself has been studied is a mystery.

Although it is a virtual certainty based on relatively recent *detective* work that Jefferson is the father of one (and likely all) of Sally Hemings' children, it appears to us that exploring this mystery is more exciting and motivating in the classroom now than it was until the end of 1998 when the paternity of her children was still an open question. A *solved* mystery touches off debates about the meaning of that mystery in the past and in the present. We could call those debates *mysteries* but that unnecessarily stretches our term. They are open-ended questions argued on historical grounds. These debates provide the impetus for going back and reviewing the evidence in the specific mystery and the wider historical context.

## Jefferson and Hemings: What is at stake?

Joseph J. Ellis stated on the *Today Show* that, "Jefferson had what is almost certainly a long-term sexual relationship with his mulatto slave, Sally Hemings" (*Jet* 1998, 4). Yes, it is exciting and titillating and interesting to many Americans to wonder about the sex life of Thomas Jefferson, and we hope that includes our students. If a little innuendo and gossip gets them to learn how to weigh evidence and use documents, then we say bravo! But there are also deep value issues that motivated people to investigate this Jefferson mystery and to consider the findings, not just voyeurism. This means that Jefferson held his own children as slaves; to some this may not be overly significant because he was undeniably a slaveholder. But to Robert Gillespie, the head of the Monticello Association, a group for the descendants of Jefferson's two daughters from his marriage to Martha Wayles, it made a considerable difference in the way he regarded his ancestor. He told *The New York Times* "that he had always believed that 'Jefferson would have shown the second set of children love and affection just as he did the first set. Apparently he was a product of the eighteenth century, and had a double standard.'" It puts Jefferson's stand against *miscegenation*—the term for blacks and whites sleeping together—in a very different light.

Discussing the significance of the DNA findings in the same issue of *Nature* that contained the scientific study, Dr. Lander, the geneticist, and Dr. Ellis, the historian, wrote that Jefferson justified his opposition to emancipation on the grounds that it would lead to interracial children. They reflect that, "His own interracial affair now personalizes this issue, while adding a dimension of hypocrisy" (Lander and Ellis 1998, 14). Students might wonder if he held this position so strongly perhaps because he himself was guilty of the very act he considered taboo. Jefferson's life personifies two parts of the slave system—that slave women were vulnerable to the sexual demands of their owners and that white families owned their children, or brothers and sisters. Raising these allegations and then tracing what became of Sally Hemings' children also complicates categories of slave and free, or black and white, since two of her children cemented their freedom by passing for white in their twenties, while two remained identified as members of the African American community until Eston Hemings and his family passed for white sometime around 1850.

Writing in the Op Ed section of *The New York Times*, Harvard sociologist Orlando Patterson hoped that "knowing that the greatest of our Founding Fathers was a practicing miscegenist should energize the recent shift away from the either–or definition of 'race' that has historically underpinned the caste-like segregation of African-Americans toward a more blended and self-chosen definition of group identity" (Patterson 1998). Students may think of black and white as categories that are not strictly a matter of biology, but also a matter of social definition and personal choice. Jefferson chose not to openly acknowledge his children with Hemings. Some of those children, who were aided tacitly or directly by Jefferson in escaping slavery, chose to arrive anonymously in a new community and portray themselves as white, which carried its own set of risks, and others remained black. None of these were *free* choices entirely up to the individual, but the circumstances that allowed them to make those choices were as much social as biological.

Studying this mystery early in a course running chronologically can provide students with a richer, more complex vocabulary to use later on when following debates over the Dredd Scott case, when trying to make sense of Reconstruction, or when discussing contemporary racial questions.

Philip Morgan argues that we should examine specific cases such as the Jefferson/Hemings relationship, and "tell the stories of individuals, not just for the human interest that such tales convey but because truth often resides in the intimate details of singular lives" (1999, 55). Agreeing with Morgan as we do means holding in mind the knowledge that we cannot generalize from a single person to a whole society, but once we have done research, it is possible to pick an individual case and discuss how that case is similar to and different from the rest of the world. If we choose to present Jefferson and Hemings, we can do so with a sense of the ways in which they represent broad patterns and truths about the past, as well as the ways in which the third President led his own life with privileges and choices unavailable to others. Ellis characterized Jefferson as "a window in which race and slavery are the panes" (1998, 1). Through our students' interest in Thomas Jefferson and Sally Hemings we can encourage them to peer back into the eighteenth and nineteenth centuries to discover something of plantation life and American society that applies beyond the boundaries of Monticello.

## (Re)constructing a mystery: From solved to whodunit

We just argued the broad significance of the Jefferson/Hemings affair, but in structuring a classroom mystery to investigate it, we can take comfort in the relative narrowness of the question, "Did Thomas Jefferson have a sexual relationship with Sally Hemings?" This is a manageable and focused question to answer compared to trying to understand an entire culture. The Jefferson/Hemings case has all of the elements of a classic *whodunit* detective novel, with questions of opportunity, eyewitness testimony, and circumstantial evidence all coming into play. While the question itself is narrow, there are mountains of evidence to consider. Much of this evidence has been gathered together in reports for the Thomas Jefferson Foundation, Inc., in scholarly publications reflecting on the DNA findings, and in the pre-DNA examination of the evidence published by law professor Annette Gordon-Reed. Interested teachers can download a PDF file or two from the Monticello website (*www.monticello.org*), or get Gordon-Reed's 1997 book and the 1999 collection of essays edited by Jan Lewis and Peter Onuf; suddenly, you'll have enough Jefferson material for an extended classroom study, some of it nearly classroom-ready.

As you consider the vast quantities of evidence, it may help you to think about your students as gumshoe detectives.

- Which witnesses will they interview?
- What evidence will they examine?
- What evidence is central to the case and what is peripheral?
- Is the evidence linked? If so, how? If not, why not?

Each item of evidence can lead to more items. Testimony by Madison Hemings about what his mother told him is corroborated by Israel Jefferson, another slave at Monticello, but contradicted by the testimony of Ellen Coolidge and Thomas Jefferson Randolph—Thomas Jefferson's grandchildren.

There is an oral history tradition in the Woodson family that Thomas Woodson was the son of Thomas Jefferson and Sally Hemings. The DNA testing did not support that claim, but there are allegations that Jefferson had an interracial son named Tom, yet cross-checking with the Farm Book, in which Jefferson recorded all such information, there is no record of such a person. Moreover, the central items of evidence span a time period of about a hundred years, from the 1780s to the 1870s. Each piece of evidence evokes new questions of context, specifically: How was that item influenced by the time period and circumstances of its creation?

In constructing this mystery and seeing where it may lead, we think that we are catching the excitement of the *decision-making* approach to social studies advocated in 1960 by Shirley Engle—a course should focus around the students themselves deciding the meaning of data. Teachers introduce data about a topic, the class forms an hypothesis, and then tests it. After getting each new bit of evidence, students revise the hypothesis and test it again, just as a detective revises his or her theories about the case with each new encounter. Engle argued that such an approach to learning about a topic would require the "introduction of vastly larger quantities of factual information into our classrooms . . . far too much content to be committed to memory" (1960, 5). Each tentative conclusion, or decision, about a given set of facts will call for more facts in order to test and refine the first decision, an ever-expanding progression. This is how we will proceed with the Jefferson/Hemings investigation.

## Did Jefferson have a sexual relationship with Hemings and father at least one of her children?

We are going to present eight items of evidence. After each item we ask how that specific item affects your thinking about the main question and ask you to rate the *mysteriousness* of that item of evidence as minor, medium, or major. After Item Three, Item Seven, and again at the end, we will interrupt your contemplation of each individual item, and ask you to consider all the previous pieces of evidence and make two judgments about the case as a whole. We also ask you about the relationship between Hemings and Jefferson and about the difficulty of the mystery. We restrict ourselves to minimal comments on each of these eight items as you encounter them. Once you have had the opportunity to examine the documents, we will review the evidence packet using the five criteria for rating a mystery. You'll find details of how to explore giving the mystery an overall rating and how to judge each particular aspect of the rating system, or just judging each item of evidence.

This chapter does not focus on presenting these materials in the classroom, but on constructing a *whodunit* for your students out of the voluminous evidence available when someone has solved a long-standing mystery. You can consider the difficulty of each individual item, deciding whether we supply enough information for students to *get* the mystery—that is, can they understand the identities of the major actors and the meaning of the key pieces of evidence on which conclusions are based? Then, consider how much or how little material you want to present in your classroom to solve this case. Will you provide less and give your students a minor mystery? Will you present less, but more difficult, material and make it a major mystery; is that possible based on the evidence here?

These are the types of questions you should consider as you sort through the eight Jefferson/Hemings items in the mystery packet. Overall, this is considered a constructed mystery because we know how it turns out and can tell students about the DNA and one or two other proofs and move on, in the manner of a newspaper reporting this story. Instead, we have manufactured, or reconstructed, this mystery. Knowing that we pieced together one possible version of the mystery gives you license to think about how you would adjust the materials to create a case for your classroom. Will students who sort through these documents have a better view of Jefferson and of the eighteenth and nineteenth centuries, as we (and Philip Morgan) think they will? Do you?

# THE JEFFERSON/HEMINGS EVIDENCE

### ITEM ONE, CALLENDER ARTICLE

It is well known that the man, whom it delighteth the people to honor, keeps and for many years has kept, as his concubine, one of his slaves. Her name is SALLY. The name of her eldest is Tom. His features are said to bear a striking though sable resemblance to those of the President himself. The boy is ten or twelve years of age. His mother went to France in the same vessel with Mr. Jefferson and his two daughters. The delicacy of this arrangement must strike every person of common sensibility. What a sublime pattern for an American ambassador to place before the eyes of two young ladies. . . . By this wench Sally our President has had several children. There is not an individual in the neighborhood of Charlottesville who does not believe the story, and not a few who know it. . . . The AFRICAN VENUS is said to officiate, as housekeeper at Monticello.

— JAMES CALLENDER, *Richmond Recorder*, 1 September 1802

This specific item suggests/makes me inclined to

_____ Accept _____ Reject_____ Remain undecided

that Jefferson had a relationship with Sally Hemings because

Mystery rating of this item: Minor\_\_\_\_\_ Medium\_\_\_\_\_ Major\_\_\_\_\_

*Short note about James Callender:* In the 1790s, he admired Thomas Jefferson and wrote anti-Federalist articles. Jefferson gave him financial support as a pro-Republican journalist, although as Callender used ever-stronger language in attacking the Federalists, Jefferson dropped him. Under the Sedition Act, the Federalists sent Callender to jail and fined him $200. Jefferson pardoned him once in office and sought to repay the fine, but refused to offer Callender a federal job. Callender began researching rumors about Jefferson, and soon started publishing attacks on the President.

## ITEM TWO, JEFFERSON AND HEMINGS FAMILY TREES

*Short note on the family trees:* These trees establish the major characters in the mystery and their relationships to each other without the need for much narrative. Remember that they are drawn up by people at Monticello now, and think of them as constructs. Ask, what do the plus signs mean next to Beverly and Harriet Hemings? The connection between the two charts is that John Wayles is both the father of Sally Hemings and of Martha Wayles Jefferson, Thomas Jefferson's wife. (See Figures 4–1 and 4–2, pp. 96–97.)

The family tree makes me included to

_____ Accept _____ Reject_____ Remain undecided

that Jefferson had a relationship with Sally Hemings because

Mystery rating of this item: Minor_____ Medium_____ Major_____

## ITEM THREE, CONCEPTION CHARTS

*Note:* There is no record that Sally Hemings was anywhere but at Monticello from 1790 to 1826. If Jefferson was away from Monticello nine months before she gave birth, he could not have been the father. Jefferson was living permanently at Monticello in 1794 and 1795 but afterward traveled and later lived in the White House during his presidency. He kept records of the dates he spent at Monticello. (See Figures 4–3a,b, p. 98.)

The conception/Jefferson-visits chart makes me inclined to

_____ Accept _____ Reject_____ Remain undecided

that Jefferson had a relationship with Sally Hemings because

Mystery rating of this item: Minor _____ Medium _____ Major_____

# Descendants of Thomas and Mary Field Jefferson*

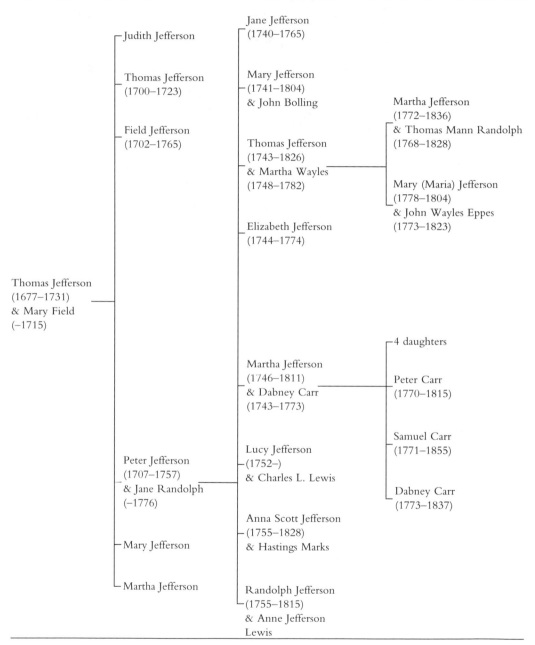

Thomas Jefferson
(1677–1731)
& Mary Field
(–1715)

Judith Jefferson

Thomas Jefferson
(1700–1723)

Field Jefferson
(1702–1765)

Jane Jefferson
(1740–1765)

Mary Jefferson
(1741–1804)
& John Bolling

Thomas Jefferson
(1743–1826)
& Martha Wayles
(1748–1782)

Elizabeth Jefferson
(1744–1774)

Martha Jefferson
(1772–1836)
& Thomas Mann Randolph
(1768–1828)

Mary (Maria) Jefferson
(1778–1804)
& John Wayles Eppes
(1773–1823)

Peter Jefferson
(1707–1757)
& Jane Randolph
(–1776)

Mary Jefferson

Martha Jefferson

Martha Jefferson
(1746–1811)
& Dabney Carr
(1743–1773)

Lucy Jefferson
(1752–)
& Charles L. Lewis

Anna Scott Jefferson
(1755–1828)
& Hastings Marks

Randolph Jefferson
(1755–1815)
& Anne Jefferson
Lewis

4 daughters

Peter Carr
(1770–1815)

Samuel Carr
(1771–1855)

Dabney Carr
(1773–1837)

*Generally acknowledged by historians prior to the DNA study.

FIG 4–1   Family Tree: Descendants of Thomas and Mary Field Jefferson.

# Descendants of Elizabeth Hemings*

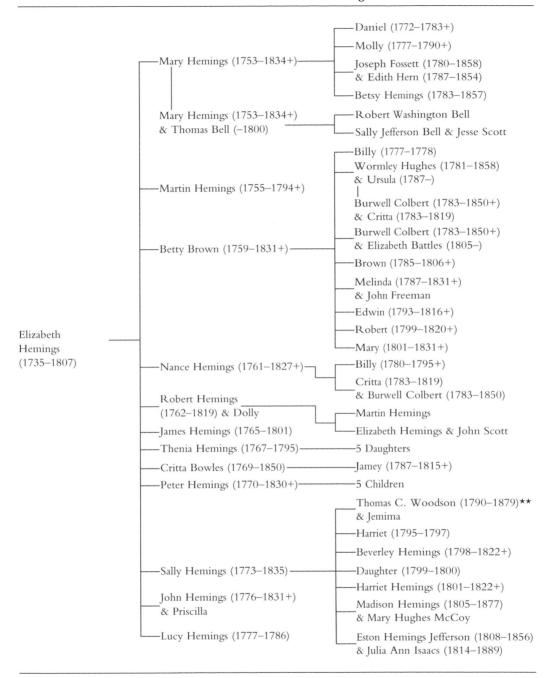

Mary Hemings (1753–1834+)
- Daniel (1772–1783+)
- Molly (1777–1790+)
- Joseph Fossett (1780–1858) & Edith Hern (1787–1854)
- Betsy Hemings (1783–1857)

Mary Hemings (1753–1834+) & Thomas Bell (–1800)
- Robert Washington Bell
- Sally Jefferson Bell & Jesse Scott

Martin Hemings (1755–1794+)

Betty Brown (1759–1831+)
- Billy (1777–1778)
- Wormley Hughes (1781–1858) & Ursula (1787–)
- Burwell Colbert (1783–1850+) & Critta (1783–1819)
- Burwell Colbert (1783–1850+) & Elizabeth Battles (1805–)
- Brown (1785–1806+)
- Melinda (1787–1831+) & John Freeman
- Edwin (1793–1816+)
- Robert (1799–1820+)
- Mary (1801–1831+)

Nance Hemings (1761–1827+)
- Billy (1780–1795+)
- Critta (1783–1819) & Burwell Colbert (1783–1850)

Robert Hemings (1762–1819) & Dolly

James Hemings (1765–1801)
- Martin Hemings
- Elizabeth Hemings & John Scott

Thenia Hemings (1767–1795) — 5 Daughters

Critta Bowles (1769–1850) — Jamey (1787–1815+)

Peter Hemings (1770–1830+) — 5 Children

Elizabeth Hemings (1735–1807)

Sally Hemings (1773–1835)
- Thomas C. Woodson (1790–1879)** & Jemima
- Harriet (1795–1797)
- Beverley Hemings (1798–1822+)
- Daughter (1799–1800)
- Harriet Hemings (1801–1822+)
- Madison Hemings (1805–1877) & Mary Hughes McCoy
- Eston Hemings Jefferson (1808–1856) & Julia Ann Isaacs (1814–1889)

John Hemings (1776–1831+) & Priscilla

Lucy Hemings (1777–1786)

*Generally acknowledged by historians prior to the DNA study.
**Connection to Sally Hemings based on Woodson family oral history.

FIG 4–2   Family Tree: Descendants of Elizabeth.

### Table I
### Dates of Jefferson's Visits to Monticello

| Arrival Date | Departure Date | Length of Visit (days) |
|---|---|---|
| January 16, 1794 | February 20, 1797 | 1,131 |
| March 20, 1797 | May 5, 1797 | 46 |
| July 11, 1797 | December 4, 1797 | 146 |
| July 3, 1798 | December 18, 1798 | 168 |
| March 8, 1799 | December 21, 1799 | 288 |
| May 29, 1800 | November 24, 1800 | 179 |
| April 5, 1801 | April 26, 1801 | 21 |
| August 2, 1801 | September 27, 1801 | 56 |
| May 8, 1802 | May 27, 1802 | 19 |
| July 25, 1802 | October 1, 1802 | 68 |
| March 11, 1803 | March 31, 1803 | 20 |
| July 24, 1803 | September 22, 1803 | 60 |
| April 5, 1804 | May 11, 1804 | 36 |
| July 27, 1804 | September 27, 1804 | 62 |
| March 17, 1805 | April 14, 1805 | 28 |
| July 18, 1805 | September 29, 1805 | 73 |
| May 9, 1806 | June 4, 1806 | 26 |
| July 24, 1806 | October 11, 1806 | 69 |
| April 11, 1807 | May 13, 1807 | 32 |
| August 5, 1807 | October 1, 1807 | 57 |
| May 12, 1808 | June 8, 1808 | 27 |

### Table II
### Birthdays and Associated Statistics for Sally Hemings' Children

| Name | Birthday | IBI (days) | Estimated conception date | Days from Jefferson's arrival to estimated conception date | Jefferson's age | Heming's age |
|---|---|---|---|---|---|---|
| Harriet 1 | October 5, 1795 | | January 11, 1795 | 360 | 53 | 22 |
| Beverly | April 1, 1798 | 909 | July 8, 1797 | −3 | 55 | 25 |
| Daughter | December 7, 1799 | 615 | March 15, 1799 | 7 | 57 | 27 |
| Harriet 2 | May 15, 1801 | 524 | August 21, 1800 | 84 | 58 | 28 |
| Madison | January 19, 1805 | 1,345 | April 27, 1804 | 22 | 62 | 32 |
| Eston | May 21, 1808 | 1,218 | August 28, 1807 | 23 | 65 | 35 |

FIG 4–3a,b  Coincidence or Causal Connection? These separate tables present the Dates of Jefferson's Visits to Monticello and Birthdays and Associated Statistics for Sally Hemings' Children.

## Midway Consideration

At this point, reviewing ITEM ONE—the charge published by James Callendar, ITEM TWO—the family trees, and ITEM THREE—the conception/Jefferson visits charts, do you think the possibility of a relationship between Jefferson and Hemings is:

___ Very likely ___ Likely ___ Don't know ___ Unlikely ___ Very unlikely

Thinking about how well my students could manage these items of evidence, I would rate the mystery of the relationship as:

_____ Minor _____ Medium _____ Major

because:

### Item four, The fate of Sally Hemings' children

Farm Book entry: Beverly Hemings [Sally's oldest son] "Beverly, ran away, [18]22." There is no evidence that Jefferson made any attempt to get Beverly back, unlike his action in other runaway cases.

Farm Book Entry: "Harriet. Sally's run, [18]22." Harriet was born in 1801. She was 21 years old.

Jefferson's will, March 1826:

> I give also to John Hemings [Sally's brother, freed in the will] the services of his two apprentices, Madison and Eston Hemings [Sally's younger sons] until their respective ages of twenty-one years, at which period, I give them their freedom: and I humbly and earnestly request of the Legistlature of Virginia a confirmation of the bequest of freedom for these servants, with permission to remain in this State, where their families and connections are. (Gordon-Reed 1997, 41)

*Note*: The Farm Book was a log Jefferson kept of events at Monticello and is a major source for information about everyday life, comings and goings, crops, and all aspects of life at his estate. As for the will, these were not the only slaves freed, but only a few others were freed and no other family unit at Monticello all attained freedom.

The fate of Sally Hemings' children leads me to

_____ Accept _____ Reject _____ Remain undecided

that Jefferson had a relationship with Sally Hemings because

Mystery rating of this item: Minor_____ Medium_____ Major_____

## ITEM FIVE, JEFFERSON AND THE ACCUSATION

There is only one known account of the subject being raised in Jefferson's presence. As Jefferson's Randolph granddaughters told biographer Henry S. Randall, Jefferson's daughter Martha Randolph, roused to indignation by Irish poet Thomas Moore's couplet linking her father with a slave, thrust the offending poem in front of him one day at Monticello. Jefferson's only response was a "hearty, clear laugh" (Randall 1865, 118–19).

Jefferson's reaction to his daughter makes me inclined to

_____ Accept _____ Reject_____ Remain undecided

that Jefferson had a relationship with Sally Hemings because

Mystery rating of this item: Minor_____ Medium_____ Major_____

## ITEM SIX, MEMOIR OF MADISON HEMINGS

Thos. Jefferson was a visitor at the "great house" of John Wales. . . . He formed the acquaintance of his daughter Martha . . . and intimacy sprang up between them which ripened into love and they were married . . . and in course of time had born to them a daughter whom they named Martha. About the time she [Jefferson's daughter] was born my mother [Sally Hemings], the second daughter of John Wales and Elizabeth Hemings was born. On the death of John Wales, my grandmother, his concubine, and her children by him fell to Martha, Thomas Jefferson's wife, and consequently became the property of Thomas Jefferson . . . who was appointed minister to France. . . . His wife died and as soon after her interment as he could attend to he left for France. . . . He had sons born to him, but they died in early infancy, so he then had but two children—Martha and Maria. The latter was left home, but afterwards was ordered to follow him to France. . . . My mother accompanied her as a body servant. . . . Their stay (my mother's and Maria's) was about 18 months. But during that time my mother became Mr. Jefferson's concubine, and when he was called back home she was enciente by him. He desired to bring my mother back to Virginia with him but she demurred. She was just starting to understand the French language

FIG 4–4  *Pike County* [Ohio] *Republican* newspaper, March 13, 1873.

well, and in France she was free, while if she returned to Virginia she would be re-enslaved. So she refused to return with him. To induce her to do so he promised her extraordinary privileges, and made a solemn pledge that her children should be freed at the age of twenty-one years. In consequence of his promise, on which she implicitly relied, she returned with him to Virginia. Soon after their arrival she gave birth to a child, of whom Thomas Jefferson was the father. It lived but a short time. She gave birth to four others, and Jefferson was the father of all of them. Their names were Beverly, Harriet, Madison (myself) and Eston—three sons and one daughter. We all became free agreeably to the treaty entered into by our parents before we were born. We all married and have raised families.

— MADISON HEMINGS' MEMOIR (March 13, 1873)<br>
in the Pike County [Ohio] Republican newspaper series<br>
entitled "Life Among the Lowly" (Gordon-Reed 1997, 245–48)<br>
(See Figure 4–4, p. 101)

The oral testimony of Madison Hemings makes me inclined to

_____ Accept _____ Reject _____ Remain undecided

that Jefferson had a relationship with Sally Hemings because

Mystery rating of this item: Minor_____ Medium_____ Major_____

### ITEM SEVEN, TESTIMONY BY THOMAS JEFFERSON'S GRANDCHILDREN

In 1874, Jefferson's grandson Thomas Jefferson Randolph wrote that every member of his family "repelled with indignation this calumny. . . . To my own knowledge and that of others sixty years ago the paternity of these parties were admitted by others." Randolph told biographer Henry S. Randall that his mother asked her sons always to defend their grandfather's character and reminded them that the Hemings who most resembled Jefferson could not have been his child, since he and Sally Hemings were "far distant from each other" for fifteen months before the birth. Randolph also told Randall that the father of Sally Hemings' children was Jefferson's nephew Peter Carr and that Carr had admitted this connection to him. Randolph's sister Ellen Coolidge gave a similar account, as heard from her brother, in a letter to her husband. She named Samuel Carr, however, instead of his brother Peter, as the father of Sally Hemings' children (1874 Randolph letter; 1868 Randall letter; 1858 Coolidge letter).

The written and reported testimony of Thomas Jefferson's grandson and granddaughter makes me inclined to

_____ Accept _____ Reject _____ Remain undecided

that Jefferson had a relationship with Sally Hemings because

Mystery rating of this item: Minor_____ Medium_____ Major_____

## Nearly-the-End Consideration

At this point, taking into account the data from Jefferson's lifetime, and testimony that has been available to historians since the 1870s, I am willing to make a preliminary judgment that a relationship between Jefferson and Hemings is:

___Very likely___Likely___Don't know___Unlikely ___Very unlikely

because:

Thinking about how well my students could manage these Items One through Seven of evidence, I would rate the mystery of the relationship as:

_____ Minor _____Medium _____Major

because:

### ITEM EIGHT, DNA EVIDENCE

There is a long-standing historical controversy over the question of US President Thomas Jefferson's paternity of the children of Sally Hemings, one of his slaves. To throw some scientific light on the dispute, we have compared Y-chromosomal DNA haplotypes from male-line descendants of Field Jefferson, a paternal uncle of Thomas Jefferson, with those of male-line descendants of Thomas Woodson, Sally Hemings putative first son, and of Eston Hemings Jefferson, her last son. . . .

Because most of the Y chromosome is passed unchanged from father to son, apart from occasional mutations, DNA analysis of the Y chromosome can reveal whether or not individuals are likely to be male-line relatives. We therefore analysed DNA from the Y chromosomes of: five male-line descendants of two sons of the President's paternal uncle, Field Jefferson; five male-line descendants of two sons of Thomas Woodson; one male-line descendant of Eston Hemings Jefferson; and three male-line descendants of three sons of John Carr, grandfather of Samuel and Peter Carr. No Y-chromosome data were available from male-line descendants of President Thomas Jefferson because he had no surviving sons. . . .

Four of the five descendants of Field Jefferson shared the same haplotype at all loci, and the fifth differed by only a single unit at one microsatellite locus, probably a mutation. This haplotype is rare in the population, where the average frequency of a microsatellite haplotype is about 1.5 percent. Indeed, it has never been observed outside the Jefferson family, and it has not been fond in 670 European men . . . typed with MSY1.

Four of the five male-line descendants of Thomas Woodson shared a haplotype . . . that was not similar to the $Y$ chromosome of Field Jefferson but was characteristic of Europeans. . . . In contrast, the descendant of Eston Hemings did have the Field Jefferson haplotype. The haplotypes of two of the descendants of John Carr were identical, the third differed by one step at one microsatellite locus and by one step in the MSY1 code. The Carr haplotypes differed markedly from those of the descendants of Field Jefferson.

The simplest and most probable explanations for our molecular findings are that Thomas Jefferson, rather than one of the Carr brothers, was the father of Eston Hemings Jefferson, and that Thomas Woodson was not Thomas Jefferson's son. The frequency of the Jefferson haplotype is less than 0.1 percent, a result that is at least 100 times more likely if the President was the father of Eston Hemings Jefferson than if someone unrelated was the father.

We cannot completely rule out other explanations of our findings based on illegitimacy in various lines of descent. For example, a male-line descendant of Field Jefferson could possibly have illegitimately fathered an ancestor of the presumed male-line descendant of Eston. But in the absence of historical evidence to support such possibilities, we consider them to be unlikely.

—FOSTER (1998, 27–28)

*Note:* The key finding here is that the distinctive haplotype found on the $Y$ chromosome of Jefferson males was also characteristic of the $Y$ chromosome of Eston Hemings' male-line descendants but not of the $Y$ chromosome of either of the Carr brothers nor of the male-line descendants of the Thomas Woodson. Eston Hemings is descended from some Jefferson male (or there was a 1.5 percent chance of mutation) and not from the Carr brothers.

The DNA evidence makes me inclined to

_____Accept  _____Reject _____Remain undecided

that Jefferson had a relationship with Sally Hemings because:

Mystery rating of this item: Minor_____  Medium_____  Major_____

## *Final Consideration*

After reviewing the eight pieces of evidence presented here, I think a relationship between Jefferson and Hemings was

___Very likely ___Likely ___Don't know ___Unlikely ___Very unlikely

Thinking about how well my students could manage these items of evidence, I would rate the mystery of the relationship as:

_____ Minor _____ Medium _____ Major

because:

# Rating the items according to five criteria for judging mysteries

By now we are curious to know how you have judged this mystery, and bursting to tell you what we have made of it. We have chosen to shape this exchange around the structure provided by our five criteria to judge a mystery. This section will help explain how we think about using the criteria, even as we get to tell you why we think that the Jefferson/Hemings case, as presented here, is a medium mystery. Applying each criterion to the eight items of evidence also allows us to examine how the items are constructed and how we reshaped them into the form you find here. We can consider parts of the items and related evidence that we omitted and how the presence of those additional parts might have tipped any of these rating scales. In addition, we can reflect on some of the responses these items evoke within us and how or whether those responses affect our judgments.

What the criteria will not do so readily is help us consider how successful we have been in constructing a satisfying mystery for students or in using the Jefferson/Hemings case to explore the larger issues of race and relationships and life in the eighteenth and nineteenth centuries. So, we will need further discussion of those matters, and of other possible material for inclusion in the mystery we create for students. That conversation about alternative constructions of the mystery, engagement with the past, and student satisfaction are the subject of Chapter 5. For now, let us turn our attention to using the five evidence criteria you have already examined.

## 1. Comprehension: Easy to medium to difficult

Some judicious editing has kept these sources relatively comprehensible. Every bit of writing excerpted in the items is actually much longer, more complex, and often is only one item in a series. Callender's original article is quite a bit longer, and he published many other articles. Other newspapers around the country responded to his charges or even elaborated on them. So this snippet from his original article making the charges stands in for a host of articles we left out. Had we included the complete material, the sheer length, Callender's vitriolic tone, and the accumulating details might have made this a major mystery.

Similarly, the actual "DNA article" is longer and more technical, and there was another round of writing in *Nature* qualifying the exact nature of the findings presented in the article we excerpted. Madison Hemings' memoir is actually several pages long, and Jefferson's granddaughter Ellen Coolidge wrote two- to four-page letters about the Hemings children from which we copied a few lines. We manufactured what we perceived to be a medium-level comprehensible version of each of the sources, aiming to retain each source's key evidence. We also kept something of the author's tone, and the contradictions between them, all the while keeping them brief enough to consider as a whole.

Now we want to raise a question about the construction of the family trees, but deciding which mystery rating criterion is the most appropriate to that question forces us to examine the rating scales themselves. We could discuss the family trees under *Reliability* but have chosen to consider them here under *Comprehension* because the family trees are so straightforward but under the prodding of a teacher they can become rather more confusing and complex, as we discuss in a moment.

First, another few words about the mystery rating scales. OK, we admit that even we, the creators of these mystery rating criteria, find them a bit arbitrary, but they do emphasize different qualities of the evidence. While the question we are raising about students' comprehension of the family trees could also be expressed as a question about the reliability of the family trees, our point is that the family trees look simple and factual; however, of course, they are simplified renderings of often complicated stories. The family trees are highly interpretative. It is interpretative to omit the Hemings' children from Jefferson's descendants, though this is acknowledged by an asterisk (*) that qualifies them on the chart as descendants "generally acknowledged by historians prior to the DNA study."

How would the charts look if they were linked, with Sally Hemings on the page next to Martha Wayles Jefferson and Harriet, Beverly, Madison, and Eston Hemings listed next to Martha and Mary Jefferson? An alternative family tree, listing the offspring of Thomas Jefferson and Sally Hemings, is shown in Figure 4–5 for you to consider, but this is not the same as a tree placing the two families—the Elizabeth Hemings family and the Thomas and Mary Field Jefferson families—together. Would you draw a different conclusion about the case with a different chart?

It is also common convention to omit the other four childern who were born to Martha Wayles Jefferson and Thomas Jefferson, besides their two daughters who lived to maturity; they had six children born to them (McLaughlin 1988, 178). Jane Randolph, born in April 1774 lived for 17 months, a son born in May 1777 lived only 17 days. There were two daughters named Lucy Elizabeth and neither child lived to be three years old; the first Lucy Elizabeth died after four and half months, and eighteen months later, May 8, 1782, Thomas and Martha Jefferson named another daughter Lucy Elizabeth. The second Lucy Elizabeth lived for two and half years before dying of whooping cough (McLaughlin 1988, 196–97). Yet, as the question of conception and fatherhood is so crucial to the Jefferson/Hemings story, two daughters of Sally Hemings who lived to age two and one, respectively, clearly appear on the Hemings family tree.

Furthermore, the dates on many of the lives appear with a plus (+) next to what should be the date of the individuals' death. This seems puzzling at first, doesn't it? In the case of Beverly and Harriet Hemings, 1822 represents the date at which they ran away from Monticello and, in order to pass as white, severed all family ties so that they are beyond the reach of historical record. The complete testimony of Madison Hemings suggests that the family knew something of their lives, and that they lived well past 1822, when they were in their early twenties. No such + signs qualify the dates on the Jefferson side of the family tree because they did not have to hide their identity to pass as white. Their birth and death dates are available because they never had to hide the *truth* about their

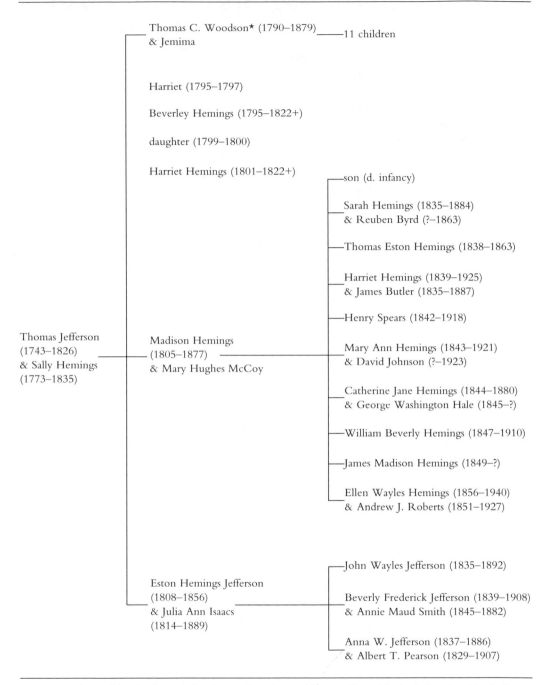

Thomas C. Woodson* (1790–1879) ——— 11 children
& Jemima

Harriet (1795–1797)

Beverley Hemings (1795–1822+)

daughter (1799–1800)

Harriet Hemings (1801–1822+)

Thomas Jefferson
(1743–1826)
& Sally Hemings
(1773–1835)

Madison Hemings
(1805–1877)
& Mary Hughes McCoy

——son (d. infancy)

Sarah Hemings (1835–1884)
& Reuben Byrd (?–1863)

Thomas Eston Hemings (1838–1863)

Harriet Hemings (1839–1925)
& James Butler (1835–1887)

Henry Spears (1842–1918)

Mary Ann Hemings (1843–1921)
& David Johnson (?–1923)

Catherine Jane Hemings (1844–1880)
& George Washington Hale (1845–?)

William Beverly Hemings (1847–1910)

James Madison Hemings (1849–?)

Ellen Wayles Hemings (1856–1940)
& Andrew J. Roberts (1851–1927)

Eston Hemings Jefferson
(1808–1856)
& Julia Ann Isaacs
(1814–1889)

John Wayles Jefferson (1835–1892)

Beverly Frederick Jefferson (1839–1908)
& Annie Maud Smith (1845–1882)

Anna W. Jefferson (1837–1886)
& Albert T. Pearson (1829–1907)

*Source*: Based on public, family, and church records and on oral history. Created by Lucia Standon, Monticello.

FIG 4–5   Hemings-Jefferson Family Tree.

family. The + signs are a reasonable choice by Monticello family-tree designers who do not know when Beverley or Harriet Hemings died, but the need for such a decision underscores the many choices (and therefore possible alternatives) involved in the construction of the family trees. They do not represent simple facts but are an interpretive presentation of a complex reality.

The complexity of the family trees is comprehensible, but helps to raise the mystery to at least a medium level, in our opinion, because the Hemings side has every birth listed while the Wayles/Jefferson side omits the majority of children Martha Wayles Jefferson delivered. The different criteria that led to the choices of how to represent the families emphasizes that interpretative decisions shaped these trees too; they do not only reflect births and deaths. We hope that students learn some healthy skepticism when they realize that family trees are not simply factual.

What do you think about our mystery rating criteria? Should we have discussed the family trees here, or under Reliability? They are not false, exactly; it is just misleading to think of them as factual, not as constructed. The conception chart is a construction as well, although in this case it straightforwardly sorts out the information obtained by cross-referencing many Farm Book entries.

The Farm Book's entries and the Will are written in plain language, but they do not so easily speak for themselves. They are straightforward because everyone agrees that they are reliable—the names and dates are accurate and the Will was not disputed at all. Both were written by Jefferson and reflect his intent. So it is a straightforward matter to get at birthdates, his visits to Monticello, and create a conception table from the Farm Book. Between the Will and the Book, we can establish that all of Sally Hemings' children achieved freedom, either by running away or by manumission in the Will. But the Book's entries are mute because "run away" does not tell the story of the circumstances behind the departures, or add that no efforts were made to recapture those slaves, or explain that Jefferson actually had his overseer buy a stagecoach ticket for Harriet Hemings that let her escape. Then, the Will is worded so that Sally Hemings' younger sons are freed as apprentices to her brother. Instead of granting their freedom directly, rather the Will grants John Hemings the "services" of his nephews as his apprentices until they turn twenty-one, "at which point I give them their freedom." The freedom bestowed on Madison and Eston Hemings in the Will reads almost as an afterthought, yet when Jefferson wrote the Will Madison Hemings had already been twenty-one for several months—Madison would never serve John Hemings at all!

Why write it that way? Did Jefferson purposely obscure the full intentions behind that grant of freedom? Can we decide? In our view these documents are easily comprehensible at face value. But, if you encourage students to ponder the construction of charts, such as the family tree, or consider the silences in the Farm Book and the Will, they are likely to find themselves in much more complicated conversations with the sources provided. The extent to which you assist, or remain neutral in such an inquiry, determines the extent to which these sources constitute a minor, medium, or major mystery. As we will discuss later, it is in pushing students to seek out these complications that you also push them to consider the multiple constructions of race that were part of the challenge of life at Jefferson's Monticello.

## 2. Reliability: Few chances for error to some to many

As we conceded when writing about the family trees, the concerns about their construction also raise issues about their reliability, arguably placing them in this category, so we mention them now. The conception charts, the Will, and the Farm Book (Items Three and Four) are also included in Reliability, but this time with an emphasis on the few chances for error they contain.

This category raises its own set of valuable questions about the trustworthiness of evidence for students to ponder. There is a chance for error even in the DNA studies. Laboratory procedures are not perfect, but there was more than one lab analyzing the blood of the Jefferson and Hemings descendants, both labs with reputations for careful work. Questioning the lab results is healthy, though in this case we are unlikely to turn up any problems. The lines of descent could themselves have errors. One unreported affair could break the male-line descent on which the study relies, and there is also the question of random mutation.

The rare haplotype found on both the Jefferson family genes and on the descendant of Eston Hemings is the key to the findings. But scientists concede that there is a possibility, even though the likelihood is less than 1 percent, that over several generations Eston Hemings' descendants could have experienced the same random mutation that Thomas Jefferson's ancestors did. That mutation would produce a match between Jefferson's family and Eston Hemings' family even though Thomas Jefferson was not Eston Hemings' father. On the whole, however, the DNA report has a relatively low probability for error since it is unlikely that there was a mistake in the work carried out by two separate laboratories and there is a less than a 1 percent chance that the match between the descendants of Eston Hemings and Field Jefferson is the result of a random mutation.

The problems with the rest of the evidence, testimony, or writing from the various characters involved in the dispute seems to us more a matter of *Viewpoint*. As was the case with the family trees, wondering which category is the best match for the questions we want to raise about a specific item of evidence reminds us that we created the categories in the first place and that deciding how to use them is a matter of judgment, not a question with a *right* answer. Keep reading and see if you agree with us that the reliability of the testimony is best discussed using the *Viewpoint* criterion. The mix of quite reliable evidence, along with evidence that has some chance for error, leads us to conclude that, on this score, the Jefferson/Hemings case is still a good medium mystery.

## 3. Viewpoint: Agreeable to conflicting to contradictory

James Callender, someone Jefferson helped support, was an enemy of Thomas Jefferson at the time he wrote the article about Jefferson and Hemings. If he could have smeared Jefferson he would have, and so Mr. Callender is probably not the most reliable of witnesses. On the other hand, there was a great deal of corroborating evidence to help him out. It appears certain that even if he did not do his own investigating or find independent proof, Callender was, at worst, reporting a tale widely discussed in Virginia. His newspaper article has a good chance of error because it was written with the intent to injure Jefferson, and may not have been thoroughly researched. On the other hand, the charge appears to have hit home, so maybe Callender was careful about obtaining as much of the story as he could based on reliable accounts.

The article needs to be treated carefully and while we have to take into account the author's viewpoint (he hated Jefferson and hoped to destroy him), its claims must be considered in relation to other evidence. There are the testimonies by Madison Hemings and the denials by Thomas Jefferson's grandchildren. Here we see two contradictory family traditions. One tradition must be wrong. We know that there must be error here. Yet that does not mean that either version is necessarily entirely correct. On the question of paternity, while there may be shades of gray as to the reliability of all parts of the testimony, this is an historical moment when students cannot say that there are two versions and the *truth* is in the middle. In this case, Jefferson either is or is not the father of one or more of Sally Hemings' children.

The stories in question contain strong elements of Viewpoint as well. Jefferson's grandchildren are denying that their grandfather had an affair with his slave and owned his children. This seems to be the likely viewpoint that a family member would take. At first glance most students would feel that Madison Hemings' testimony is a mirror-image of Viewpoint, that we all would like to claim a measure of greatness through our connection to President Jefferson. But there is reason for some caution here. Madison Hemings was the slave of Thomas Jefferson and knew him well. Perhaps he was not so eager to be the son of the man who held his family in bondage and never acknowledged his children openly.

The extreme nature of the contradiction between the accounts given by Madison Hemings and those given by Jefferson's grandchildren argues that this is a major mystery, although we have minimized this element by our editing, giving students only a little taste of the complete and contradictory family testimonies.

## 4. Solution: Quick work to moderate to extensive study

The Jefferson/Hemings mystery presents us with a variety of information to process. Yet we lack a direct statement either from Thomas Jefferson, or from Sally Hemings, testifying to the existence of the relationship or its nature. We do have direct testimony from Madison Hemings and testimony from Jefferson's granddaughter and grandson. We have the information recorded in the Farm Book and the Will, and now we have the DNA test results. A key queston: Is this enough information to determine the answer, or is this a mystery with gaps?

In our opinion, if you do not linger too long over the evidence, worrying about the construction of the family trees, possible breaks in male-line descent, or demand to see the rest of the Will to ascertain which other slaves were freed, this mystery is solvable as presented. The evidence of some special treatment of the Hemings' children, the presence of Thomas Jefferson at Monticello during the conception period of each of Sally Hemings' children (or his failure to be absent which would make him definitely not the father), and the DNA tests—backed by Madison's oral testimony and the persistent rumors raised by Callender—support the theory of a sexual relationship. Anyone reading it the other way—that all of the evidence in favor of the sexual relationship is circumstantial/inconclusive; that Jefferson never acknowledged Harriet, Beverly, Madison, and Eston Hemings as his children; and that his acknowledged family denied it—has a basis to make that claim.

This is a mystery that is empirically solvable. You need to make a judgment about the students in your classroom, but, in general, we think that quick work will not be sufficient to engage the contradictions and search out corroboration among the eight items of evidence. However, these sources are too heavily edited to stand up to extensive study. Again, we think that for most classes a moderate effort will lead to a solution.

### 5. Issues: Informational to interpretational to theoretical

This is a category in need of further explication, but the eight items of evidence do not help us here. Most of the material in the items is informational (facts); it needs to be read carefully for the evidence that can be corroborated and held up against other evidence. Since the DNA result is straightforward, very little theoretical understanding is necessary, and although genetics is one kind of theory, that is not precisely what we had in mind for this category either.

This criterion asks us to consider both the evidence and ourselves. How trustworthy is this evidence? Is it all presented from one strong perspective or another? How confident are we in our ability to read it clearly? Can we see what is there or are we too committed to a position to consider the evidence completely?

What motives did Madison Hemings have in telling his tale to the newspaper editor during Reconstruction, when Madison was sixty-eight? What were the motives of the editor of a partisan, Republican newspaper identified with the radical Republican wing of the party in starting a feature series ("Life Among the Lowly") about the elderly African Americans in Pike County, Ohio? How did he find Madison Hemings? It is quite clear that the explicit motivation of Jefferson's grandchildren was to deny the possibility that Jefferson was the father of any of Sally Hemings' children, and they spoke to their grandfather's official biographer. How should we take that into account in our interpretation of their evidence?

Annette Gordon-Reed, author of *Thomas Jeffferson and Sally Hemings: An American Controversy,* demonstrates that over the past hundred years most historians gave the testimony of the Jefferson grandchildren more credence than the testimony of a former slave for reasons that seem biased now. Worse, she shows that they frequently dismissed Madison Hemings without careful attention to his testimony and how much could be corroborated. How open-minded are we? How willing are we to read the evidence in either direction? How does any interpretation (reasoning) conflict with ideas about race that we may (even unconsciously) cherish? How will the interaction between our current values and the values of all of the principals who provided evidence interact as we try to reach a conclusion?

## *Concluding words about the rating scales*

In considering the eight items of evidence using the five rating scales, we have explained why we think we have produced a medium mystery, and explore how we used extensive editing to achieve that goal. As the teacher, you can adjust that balance by editing down to fewer pieces of evidence or by looking in greater detail at more evidence. In the following chapter, we consider the benefits of including several varieties of additional evidence, including the work of historians, as a means for more fully exploring this mystery and more completely engaging the broader questions it raises.

# Resources

BETTS, EDWIN MORRIS, ed. 1987. *Thomas Jefferson's Farm Book*. Charlottesville, VA/London: University Press of Virginia.

ELLIS, J. 1998. "HEADLINE: DNA Test Finds Evidence of Jefferson Child by Slave." *New York Times* (1 November).

ENGLE, SHIRLEY. 1960. "Decision Making: The Heart of Social Studies Instruction." *Social Education* (24 November): 301–306.

FORUM 2000, January. "Thomas Jefferson and Sally Hemings Redux." *The William and Mary Quarterly, Series III*. 57(1): 121–210.

FOSTER, EUGENE A., ET AL. 1998. "Jefferson Fathered Slave's Last Child." *Nature*, 196 (5 November): 27-28.

GORDON-REED, ANNETTE. 1997. *Thomas Jefferson and Sally Hemings: An American Controversy*. Charlottesville, VA/London: University Press of Virginia.

JET. 1998. "U.S. President Thomas Jefferson Fathered Child with Slave, DNA Study Shows." (16 November).

LANDER, ERIC S., AND JOSEPH ELLIS. 1998. "Founding Father." *Nature*, 196 (5 November): 13-14.

LEWIS, JAN, AND PETER ONUF, eds. 1999. *Sally Hemmings and Thomas Jefferson: History, Memory, and Civic Culture*. Charlottesville, VA/London: University Press of Virginia.

McLAUGHLIN, JACK. 1988. *Jefferson and Monticello*. New York: Henry Holt and Company.

MORGAN, PHILLIP. 1999. "Interracial Sex in the Chesapeake." In Jan Lewis and Peter Onuf, eds., *Sally Hemings and Thomas Jefferson: History, Memory, and Civic Culture*. Charlottesville, VA/London: University Press of Virginia.

PATTERSON, ORLANDO. 1998. "Rituals of Blood: Consequences of Slavery in Two American Centuries." *New York Times* (2 November): Op Ed Page.

RANDALL, HENRY. 1865 (reprint 1972). *The Life of Thomas Jefferson*. New York: Derby and Jackson.

RESEARCH COMMITTEE ON THOMAS JEFFERSON AND SALLY HEMINGS. 2000.

*Majority Report of the Research Committee on Thomas Jefferson and Sally Hemings.* Monticello, VA: Thomas Jefferson Memorial Foundation; available from website.

WALLENBORN, WHITE MCKENZIE. 1999. *DNA Study Committee Minority Report.* Monticello, VA: Thomas Jefferson Memorial Foundation.

*Note:* A number of the secondary sources also reproduce key primary sources, such as the memoir of Madison Hemings.

# 5

## *Beyond the Bare Facts*
### *Exploring Race and History Through Jefferson and Hemings*

History is, of course, a science, but not one of the common type. Unlike the ordinary scientists, the scientific historian has to practice, not self-suppression, but self-expansion. He must become conscious, so far as that is possible, of the prejudices and special interests of his own age and, divested of them, he must migrate into a strange land in order to bring back thence a report that is at once an unbiased account of what he has seen as a story that is comprehensible to his fellow-citizens, or, at least, to his fellow-historians. He dare not treat the past as one in spirit with the present, or as re-solvable into precisely the same factors. He must be alive to the existence of many different pasts leading to the present in no predeterminable succession, much less progression. The points must make a line, but the line may be of any conceivable curve.

—WILLIAM S. FERGUSON, 1875–1954 (1962, 134)

## From solving a mystery to meeting a world

Did Thomas Jefferson have a sexual relationship with Sally Hemings? The last chapter provided eight items of evidence that, in our opinion, allows students to investigate that question with a fair chance of arriving at a solution. We included enough evidence for students to understand why most people now believe they did have such a relationship. Yet we also provided details about the limitations of the DNA testing, the traditions that denied Jefferson's paternity of any Hemings' child, and the muteness of Jefferson's Farm Book. Pupils who study the material can also understand, and perhaps agree with, those people who find the proofs of the relationship too circumstantial for a conclusive answer. In our discussion of the evidence, we explained why we think we created a medium mystery for the classroom, and how we edited or omitted sources in order to create a solvable, medium mystery.

In this chapter, we need to consider how well the Jefferson/Hemings mystery that we constructed helps us toward the more challenging goals we set at the beginning of the last chapter. We quoted Phillip Morgan who urges us to find truths about the past in the particular details of individual lives and we asked: "Will students who sort through these documents have a better view of Jefferson and of the eighteenth and nineteenth centuries?" We quoted Orlando Patterson who suggests that a review of the Jefferson/Hemings case would help students realize that race is not simply a black or white category, and that it is not strictly bio-logical, since Jefferson's children were considered black in some contexts and passed for white in others.

Having examined the case we constructed in Chapter 4 we now need to measure it against our intentions. Did that eight-item mystery push students to examine and reshape their thinking about race as a category? Did they (re)evaluate Thomas Jefferson as a person? Did we use the case of Jefferson and Hemings to transport ourselves back into the past, and emerge with a sense of the broader world of the late eighteenth and early nineteenth centuries when the question of a Jefferson/Hemings affair was first raised? What have students learned about the nature of history?

We suggest that the medium mystery succeeds only medium-well in con-necting students back to the eighteenth century. The materials we presented opened up many questions, but carried too great a burden of explaining the cir-cumstances of the Jefferson/Hemings mystery to allow as much exploration of their lives as we would have liked. For example, the quotation we offered from Madison Hemings, as long as it was, presented bare-bones details of his mother's circumstances as he understood them, and how she and Jefferson became inti-mate in France. Yet the memoir continues with details about Madison's escaped brother and sister, and covers his own view of Thomas Jefferson. Consider the following two paragraphs from Madison Hemings' memoir, paragraphs which we edited *out* of the eight-item mystery.

> Beverly [Hemings, Madison's brother] left Monticello and went to Washington as a white man. He married a white woman in Maryland, and their only child, a daughter, was not known by the white folks to have any colored blood coursing in her veins. Beverly's wife's family were people in good circumstances.
>
> Harriet married a white man in good standing in Washington City, whose name I could give, but will not, for prudential reasons. She raised a family of children, and so far as I know they were never suspected of being tainted with African blood in the community where she lived or lives. I have not heard from her for ten years, and do not know whether she is dead or alive. (Gordon-Reed 1997, 246)

These selections do not bear directly on the mystery of Thomas Jefferson and Sally Hemings, but they explicitly let us back into "the complicated history of mixed-race Americans, ones for whom racial identification might be a matter of personal choice" (Lewis and Onuf 1999, 4). Had we provided the students with the complete memoir of Madison Hemings, they would have encountered a com-plex discussion of Madison's grandmother Elizabeth Hemings' parentage and of her relationship with Jefferson's father-in-law John Wayles; a reflection on Thomas Jefferson as a father to his slave offspring compared to his behavior as the grand-father of white offspring; an account of growing up at Monticello; and a tale of practicing carpentry and moving West. A long, unedited document, such as Madison Hemings' memoir, might be too much for many students, but motivated by the Jefferson/Hemings mystery some might comb through it for tidbits related to Thomas Jefferson and Sally Hemings. During such a search of the memoir, those students would encounter a wider portion of the past than the one we provide in Chapter 4.

The next section of this chapter provides material that is directly connected to the Jefferson/Hemings mystery in one fashion or another, but also provides a window to more of the eighteenth-century world. Extending the medium mystery, and turning it into a major mystery through the addition of some complex and contradictory evidence, requires more classroom time and more concentration by students. At the cost of more time and complexity, these additional mystery materials bring your students into more direct contact with the multiracial world of Monticello.

Rather than present each separate item of evidence for you to analyze as you did in the previous chapter, we have grouped the new materials we would like you to examine into two additional Mystery Packets. The first considers the fate of Sally Hemings' children and the second provides materials concerning Madison Hemings' memoirs. This material has been grouped together for two purposes.

The first purpose is intellectual coherence. As you construct a case with more and more evidence, there is danger that you or your students will be overwhelmed by the evidence. The eight original items of evidence formed a backbone for this investigation, an introductory packet if you like. These additional Mystery Packets are more narrowly focused on specific questions—one on the fate of the Hemings' children and one on corroborating Madison Hemings' memoir. If we jumped from eight to fifteen items of evidence in the case, we might lose track of what we are doing. Instead, we have moved from a single packet touching on all aspects of the case, to two additional Mystery Packets that look in greater depth at Item Four (fate of Hemings' children) and Item Six (Madison Hemings' memoir) of the material in Chapter 4.

The second purpose, served by grouping the additional materials into two packets, is to enable you to divide students into groups. This is how we have managed this evidence with our students. While we want the entire class to review the eight primary items of evidence, we often distribute additional packets to smaller groups, or teams of students. This allows us to keep each set of students focused on their subquestion, and to have students working on each package simultaneously instead of having to proceed item by item with the entire class, although students might present their findings to the entire class when done. However, it might be that simply looking at one packet in addition to the eight items of primary evidence serves your teaching purpose. Organizing the additional material into packets allows for a flexible approach to expanding the mystery. If the detective image is helpful, think of this as an investigation in which more evidence has turned up!

Procedurally, we have chosen not to evaluate each item according to the five criteria for rating the difficulty of a mystery, and we will not ask you to rate them either. Knowing at the outset that we gauged the mystery created through the first eight items to be a medium mystery, you can understand why we think the expansion to fifteen items, including some complex pieces of evidence, creates a major mystery. Instead, we would like to review each of the two added Mystery Packets in terms of the opportunity it offers students to further understand the world of Monticello, or some other aspect of the past.

# MYSTERY PACKET 1

## THE FATE OF THE HEMINGS CHILDREN

1. A list of all slaves freed in Jefferson's Will (March 1826):

    - Burwell Colbert—Jefferson's personal valet for several years; Jefferson had promised he would free him (Gordon-Reed 1997, 38).

    - John Hemings—Sally Hemings' youngest brother who had been the master carpenter at Monticello.

    - John Fossett—a master ironworker at Monticello in charge of Jefferson's metal shop.

    - Madison and Eston Hemings—the youngest two living children of Sally Hemings.

2. Jefferson's granddaughter, Ellen Coolidge, wrote in 1858 that "three young men and one girl," who were "sufficiently white to pass for white," were allowed "to withdraw quietly from the plantation; it was called running away, but they were never re-claimed" (Ellen Coolidge 1858 letter).

3. Edmund Bacon 1861 Account (Jefferson's overseer at Monticello for the years 1806–1824):

    > He freed one girl some years before he died, and there was a great deal of talk about it. She was nearly as white as anybody, and very beautiful. People said he freed her because she was his own daughter. She was not his daughter; she was " . . .'s" daughter. I know that. I have seen him come out of her mother's room many a morning when I went up to Monticello very early. When she was nearly grown, by Mr. Jefferson's direction I paid her stage fare to Philadelphia and gave her fifty dollars. I have never seen her since, and don't know what became of her. From the time she was large enough, she always worked in the cotton factory. She never did any hard work.

*Note*: Pierson prepared the book himself, Bacon probably did not make the decision to publish it. Pierson wrote that while preparing the book "an utterly causeless and wicked rebellion has culminated in the establishment of the so-called Confederate State . . . the home of Thomas Jefferson has been confiscated, because its owner [Uriah P. Levy] is loyal to the Stars and Stripes. The banner of treason—the Confederate flag—now waves over the bones of the author of the Declaration of Independence." Pierson and Bacon were pro-Jefferson and antisecession, perhaps reason enough to tell this story without admitting that Jefferson had had a relationship with Hemings. If any students pay attention to the chronology, they will discover that Bacon was *not* yet at Monticello when Harriet Hemings was conceived, so he is an eyewitness to her departure, not to her parentage. He was working at Monticello when Eston Hemings was born in 1808. The circumstances surrounding the decision Bacon made to publish this story during the Civil War makes it a layered story that exemplifies the problems of an information-rich, value-laden narrative. What, in 1860, was he willing to say about Jefferson?

4. Excerpt from Memoirs of Israel Jefferson (*Pike County* [Ohio] *Republican*, 25 December 1873):

> Mr. Jefferson died on the 4th day of July, 1826, when I was upwards of twenty-nine years of age. His death was an affair of great moment and uncertainty to us slaves, for Mr. Jefferson provided for the freedom of seven servants only: Sally, his chambermaid, who took the name Hemings, her four children—Beverly, Harriet, Madison and Eston—John Hemmings, brother to Sally, and Burrel Colburn, an old and faithful body servant. Madison Hemings is now a resident of Ross County, Ohio, whose history you gave in the *Republican* of March 13, 1873. All the rest of us were sold from the auction block, by order of Jefferson Randolph, his grandson and administrator. The sale took place in 1829, three years after Mr. Jefferson's death . . . (Gordon-Reed 1997, 249–53)

### You Decide

- Do any of the four items in this additional packet teach students something important about the eighteenth/nineteenth century that they would not have learned with the primary items?
- How much additional class time would examining this package as part of the Jefferson/Hemings' mystery consume?
- Is the additional understanding worth the extra time? For what kind of students or classes? For which of your teaching goals?

# The fate of Sally Hemings' children:
# A broader encounter with the past

The selections in this package portray life at Monticello with an immediacy lacking in the initial eight items. The last selection, Israel Jefferson's memoir, is the most powerful example. While the Hemings children were secure in their freedom, which is all we learn from the initial evidence, Israel Jefferson tells us what happens to the rest of the slaves; after three years they were auctioned off to the highest bidder. Presumably families were separated, although this is not explicit in his testimony. The constraints of focusing on the Jefferson/Hemings case prevented us from including his next three sentences. In the first sentence Israel Jefferson names his purchaser, his first wife (a fellow slave), and his four children from that marriage. Here are the next two sentences: "As they [his four children] were born slaves they took the usual course of most others in the same condition of life. I do not know where they now are, if living; but the last I heard of them they were in Florida and Virginia" (Gordon-Reed 1997, 250). We do not think it is an accident that Israel Jefferson followed the story of the auction at Monticello with the story of his separation from his own children. He experienced the breakup of his family and entire community once at Monticello and another time when he was separated from his two sons and two daughters.

Even though students would not have this information, the image of the auction block is chilling enough. Thomas Jefferson began recording in his Farm Book when he owned 52 slaves, and he inherited another 135 slaves from his father-in-law in 1773 (McLaughlin 1988, 103). After more than fifty years together, the community was split by two major auctions, one in January 1827 when about 100 slaves were sold and one in 1829. The records from the 1829 sale list the names of thirty slaves who were sold, and researchers at Monticello believe that is a complete list. Since the names of Israel Jefferson's family members are not on that list, they were probably sold in the 1827 auction. Even without knowing the exact number of slaves sold at both auctions, the testimony of Israel Jefferson makes plain that the seven slaves freed by Thomas Jefferson was a small number compared to the majority of the slaves who knew that they were likely to be sold and endured anxious years and the disaster of auctions. The information presented in the list of slaves freed in the Will and corroborated in Israel Jefferson's testimony is pertinent to the mystery. Knowing who else Jefferson freed from the plantation in his Will, and how few, underscores how unusual Sally Hemings and her children were. But the importance in this evidence lies in the way Israel Jefferson's testimony pulls students into the life of slaves at the Monticello plantation, and elsewhere.

The letter from Ellen Coolidge dovetails with her comments about the Carr brothers. She did not deny that slave owners and slaves at Monticello had sexual relationships, she merely denied that Thomas Jefferson was involved in them. She was aware of multiple interracial families and of the decision to let some of the children slip away. She did not witness these events herself, but heard about them via the family oral tradition. This letter belongs in Mystery Packet 1 because it corroborates Madison Hemings' story about his sister Harriet's departure into a white life. The significance of the letter lies in its matter-of-fact acknowledgment by the Jefferson family that "Jefferson's Monticello was a mixed-race community, inhabited not only by whites and dark-skinned African Americans but also by a significant number of light-skinned slaves who were related to Jefferson in one way or another" (Lewis and Onuf 1999, 5). The story of the "three young men and one girl" who were "white enough to pass for white" tacitly admits that there is no absolute category of *white* but that it was an arbitrary line. The white family acknowledges that at Monticello slave and free were precise legal categories but the racial categories they supposedly reflected were more fictitious, and that there were "Jeffersons" who were slaves and "Jeffersons" who were free.

Edmund Bacon offers a complicated testimony that draws us into the intricate details of life at Monticello and the surrounding community. His testimony directly addresses the Jefferson/Hemings case. He gave his testimony to Pierson and did not have control over the published manuscript; his original manuscript has never been found. He wrote that many mornings he had seen a person, not Jefferson, emerging from Sally Hemings' bedroom. His is explicit that the person, whose name Bacon may have provided but Pierson never printed, and *not* Thomas Jefferson, was the father of Harriet Hemings. This is direct evidence, and perhaps misinformation, about the case, and it is not included simply to draw students into the past.

We are lucky that this key evidence also serves our purpose of drawing students into the world of Monticello. Two other parts of Bacon's statement bear directly on the eighteenth-century community around Monticello. First, the whole story of the *escape* that was not an escape is intriguing. At Jefferson's direction Bacon gave $50 and a ticket on a stagecoach to a young woman who was a slave. Jefferson's direct involvement may suggest that this was an important personal matter and students might infer, as many did at the time according to Bacon, that this slave was Jefferson's daughter. We want to stress Thomas Jefferson's behind-the-scenes planning that sent Bacon, not Jefferson, to Harriet Hemings, buying her a ticket and giving her the money for her trip.

Second, the social world at Monticello and in the rest of Albermarle County, Virginia, comes through in Bacon's recollection that there was "a great deal of talk about it." There was a fair amount of open gossip about Thomas Jefferson and Sally Hemings in 1822, the year Harriet Hemings left. Sexual relationships between master and slave may have been taboo, but it was not off-limits to gossip. *Overhearing*, two hundred years later, conversations about owners sleeping with slaves is a "juicy" introduction to the intimate world of a plantation and the surrounding county.

This additional information does not alter the basic evidence of the Farm Book or Jefferson's Will, or of Coolidge's comments on Jefferson and Hemings; it provides students with a broader historical record. These materials will not tell them explicitly that Jefferson opposed freeing female slaves, or that he had a precise mathematical formula for determining when someone became racially white. It will, perhaps, make the case of Harriet Hemings stand out as the only young woman among the slaves freed by Jefferson. Certainly the Coolidge and Bacon pieces together give a fuller picture of life in and around Monticello and make plain that people speculated out loud about the relationship between Thomas Jefferson and his slaves. Recalling our formula for looking at the introductory materials, these sources may not make them more likely to either accept or reject the proposition that Jefferson had a relationship with Hemings. They do connect the specific mystery to broader questions of attitudes toward interracial liaisons on the eve of the Civil War, multiple families on plantations, what could be spoken aloud about interracial liaisons, and the reality of slave sales.

Mystery Packet 2 contains more of the Israel Jefferson memorial, notably the portion that touches directly on the Jefferson/Hemings question, and it contains three other references, including an early twentieth-century source. Together, these items provide a greater context for thinking about Monticello and for tracing the fate of the children of the plantation into the late nineteenth century.

# MYSTERY PACKET 2

### Corroborating Madison Hemings

1. 1870—Madison Hemings was described as Jefferson's son by an Ohio census taker (U.S. Census, Ross County, Ohio).

2. Two late-nineteenth-century newspaper accounts, recalling events from the time of Eston Hemings' 1837–1852 residence in Chillicothe, referred to local rumor that he was the son of Thomas Jefferson.

   a. One noted that he bore a "striking resemblance" to Jefferson, had hair with "a tint of auburn," and was over six feet tall. Eston Hemings' entry in the *Virginia Free Register*, in 1832, recorded his height as 6'1" (*Chillicothe Leader*, 26 January 1887; Albemarle County Minute Book, 1832–1843, 12).

   b. A second article recalled that in the 1840s five white residents of Chillicothe, Ohio, were struck by the resemblance of Eston Hemings to the statue of Jefferson they had seen in Washington, DC (*Scioto Gazette*, 1902).

3. Excerpts from Memoir of Israel Jefferson (*Pike County* [Ohio] *Republican*, 25 December, 1873):

   > I was born at Monticello, the seat of Thos. Jefferson, third President of the United States, December 25—Christmas Day in the morning. The year, I suppose, was 1797. My earliest recollections are the exciting events attending the preparations of Mr. Jefferson and other members of his family on their removal to Washington, DC, where he was to take upon himself the responsibilities of the Executive of the United States for four years.
   >
   > My mother's name was Jane. She was a slave of Thomas Jefferson's and was born and always resided at Monticello till about five years after the death of Mr. Jefferson. She was sold, after his death, by the administrator, to a Mr. Joel Brown, and was taken

to Charlottesville, where she died in 1837. She was the mother of thirteen children, all by one father, whose name was Edward Gillette. . . .

The private life of Thomas Jefferson, from my earliest rememberances, in 1804, till the day of his death, was very familiar to me. For fourteen years I made the fire in his bedroom and private chamber, cleaned his office, dusted his books, run of errands and attended him bout home. . . . I know that it was a general statement among the older servants at Monticello, that Mr. Jefferson promised his wife, on her death bed, that he would not again marry. I also know that his servant, Sally Hemings (mother to my old friend and former companion at Monticello, Madison Hemings) was employed as his chamber-maid, and that Mr. Jefferson was on the most intimate terms with her; that, in fact, she was his concubine. This I know from my intimacy with both parties, and when Madison Hemings declares that he is a natural son of Thomas Jefferson, the author of the Declaration of Independence, and that his brothers Beverly and Eston and sister Harriet are of the same parentage I can as concientiously confirm his statement as any other fact which I believe from circumstances but do not positively know.

*Note*: The Israel Jefferson testimony is a nice counterpoint to Bacon's. Neither Israel Jefferson nor Bacon were present or aware of Thomas Jefferson's relationship with Sally Hemings at the time she bore most of her children, though both were there in 1808 when Eston was born. Bacon would have been in his second year on the job, and Israel Jefferson would have been eleven. Yet each had a close relationship with Thomas Jefferson in later years, close enough to have seen who was emerging from a night in the bed of a household servant. Bacon asserts it was *not* Thomas Jefferson, while Israel Jefferson asserts it *was* Thomas Jefferson. One is wrong. Who? And both extrapolate backward from their experience in a later time to what must have happened a decade or two earlier.

## Corroborating Madison Hemings: A broader encounter with the past

The Israel Jefferson quotation fills in more of the story excerpted in the brief quotation from Mystery Packet 1. This portion provides the story of his mother, sold away quite late in life from the only place she had lived, and separated from some of her children. It also provides the detailed language of making the fire, dusting books—language that shows students, who are looking with a careful eye, the inescapable intimacy of slave and owner. The reference to older servants passing down lore about family history, and Israel Jefferson's assertion of close ties to both Sally Hemings and Thomas Jefferson, demonstrate the network of conversation and relationships that knit a plantation community together. Israel Jefferson's presence in Ohio near the Hemings family seems unlikely to be coincidence, and students may pick up on this detail as well. This packet illustrates how, in pursuit of a specific mystery, students must absorb a wealth of details about the world in which that mystery is located, and the terms on which people conducted their daily lives.

The census information is the only new historical source introduced in Packet 2; the rest is newspaper accounts of testimony. The centerpiece of this packet is the account of Israel Jefferson, but the first two items of evidence are also interesting as clues to how small communities functioned. The mark on the census sheet predates the newspaper story by several years, so it demonstrates that whatever motives the editor of the *Pike County Republican* newspaper had in publishing Madison Hemings' memoir during Reconstruction, this was not a new claim Madison Hemings was suddenly making in 1873. Gordon-Reed (1997) suggests that a friendship between the census taker and the newspaper editor may explain how a reporter knew the story existed in the first place.

The two newspaper accounts are reminiscences of tales about Eston Hemings. They are second- and third-hand, but the descendants of Eston Hemings are the ones whose DNA matched up with Field Jefferson's descendants, so it is nice to include them. Historically, they show students how amazement from an 1840 trip can be remembered and printed up sixty years later! We might think of this as a *lapsed* memory that was in historical limbo for more than half a century and then *recovered* to the public at the beginning of the next century. Understanding how these stories and memories can be transmitted over the years will help students who inquire further appreciate the "Getting Word" project that was initiated by the Thomas Jefferson Foundation, Inc., to capture the oral traditions and memories of people alive now whose ancestors were slaves at Monticello.

## Historians' writings: Another source of mystery

We hope that the additional Mystery Packets provide a methodology for expanding an initial mystery, and that we have shown how the new material meets the challenge of bringing students more fully into the past. Now we want to address another challenge we set ourselves during our first discussion of *solved* mysteries.

We argue that even when new information is uncovered and a mystery is solved, we can still investigate as a mystery the way that previous historians studied the past. Why did they reach the *right* or *wrong* solution to the mystery?

In the case of Thomas Jefferson and Sally Hemings, the record suggests that Thomas Jefferson's most prestigious biographies were racially biased and also ignored the evidence in favor of *character*. Almost all biographers concluded that Jefferson could not have slept with Sally Hemings or fathered her children by relying on the letters of his white grandchildren while discounting Madison Hemings' memoir. As we will see, what many said about his character is also unrelated to the evidence, yet many found it conclusive. In the Jefferson/Hemings case, Annette Gordon-Reed of the New York Law School has written most carefully about how historians have treated each item of evidence in the case, and the points we make here are ones she has already made in greater detail. Since her book, *Thomas Jeffreson and Sally Hemings: An American Controversy*, is organized by the different items of evidence, it is an excellent source if you want to have students compare their interpretation of the evidence with the way earlier historians interpreted any specific item of evidence (Gordon-Reed 1997). We will proceed in a different, and more cursory fashion. Our goal is to consider the viewpoint these historians brought to their work.

Here we examine brief excerpts from the work of three generations of Jefferson scholars who said that there was never a relationship. In this investigation, the emphasis is not on the judgment they reached, but on the reasoning behind that judgment. Merril Peterson published *The Jefferson Image in the American Mind* in 1960; the study was not a biography, but it provided a history of the way Americans had thought about Jefferson. Peterson still wrote about Jefferson in the book, since he often contrasted what happened in his life with the way later generations of Americans represented Jefferson's life and thought. Dumas Malone published a six-volume biography of Thomas Jefferson, collectively entitled *Jefferson and His Time*. He and Peterson were contemporaries, but Malone addressed the Jefferson/Hemings case a decade later in the fourth volume—*Jefferson the President, First Term*—published in 1970. Joseph Ellis' 1998 biography, *American Sphinx*, is the last major study published before the results of the DNA tests. The next section presents excerpts from all three books that deal with the case and Madison Hemings' memoir specifically. After some discussion of the way they dealt with the evidence provided by Madison Hemings, we again present excerpts, this time from Malone and Ellis, about the character of Thomas Jefferson, again followed by discussion.

## Excerpts from three historians

As you review these excerpts, we suggest you ask the following questions:

1. Does the author seriously consider Madison Hemings' testimony?
2. If the author rejects the testimony, does he give a reason? What is that reason? Does it seem to be a reason from a system of weighing evidence or from racial bias?

**EXCERPTS FROM MERRILL PETERSON**   Merrill Peterson discusses the Jefferson/ Hemings case in *The Jefferson Image in the American Mind* in the "Union" chapter— how people on all sides of the debate over slavery and then the Civil War used Jefferson to make their case. He attributes the perpetuation of the Jefferson/Hemings story to abolitionists who used the story to attack the institution of slavery.

> [T]he legend of miscegenation . . . lives to this day, though the crucial role of the abolitionists in its history seems to have been forgotten. . . . While there was not much evidence tending to prove the legend, neither was their positive disproof. Jefferson himself had never made a denial. (1960, 181)

Peterson cited the T. J. Randolph letter denying the relationship, and Edmund Bacon's denial, while acknowledging Israel Jefferson's testimony that Jefferson and Hemings did have a relationship and that Thomas Jefferson was the father of her children. Peterson devoted two pages to Madison Hemings:

> More credible than anything that survives are the recollections of Madison Hemings. . . . Madison's memories of Jefferson at Monticello were vivid and accurate. . . . The recollection checks remarkably well with the data accumulated by scholars on Jefferson's domestic life and the Monticello slaves. But it does not prove that Sally was Jefferson's concubine or Madison his son. Paternity, of course, is one of the most difficult things in the world to prove. It will probably never be proven in this case. The legend survives, although no serious student of Jefferson has ever declared his belief in it. (1960, 185–86)

Peterson attributed the survival of this "legend" in part to the effects of slavery:

> the Negroes' pathetic wish for a little pride and their subtle ways of confounding the white folks, the cunning of the slave trader . . . who might expect a better price for a Jefferson . . . and, above all, the logic of abolitionism. . . . (1960, 187)

**EXCERPTS FROM DUMAS MALONE**   Dumas Malone wrote about the Jefferson/ Hemings case in *Jefferson the President, First Term* as he recounted James Callender's attack on Jefferson during his first term in office, and also in an appendix at the end. These selections are from the book's appendix. This sentence claims that Sally Hemings received special consideration because she was Martha Jefferson's half-sister. We will consider this explanation later in the chapter.

> [Explaining why he freed the Sally Hemings family] Jefferson, shouldered and bore quietly for half a century the grievous burden of responsibility for the illegitimate half brothers and sisters of his own adored wife. (1970, 497)

Malone mentioned Madison Hemings' biography in a footnote of the appendix:

> While the autobiography checks with known facts in the case in certain respects it is clearly erroneous in others, and one can argue that Sally's claim, if made, may be

attributed to vanity. At all events, it must be weighed against the testimony of Jefferson's grandchildren, his categorical denial of the alleged liaison, and his own character. (1970, 498)

EXCERPTS FROM JOSEPH ELLIS   Ellis wrote about the Jefferson/Hemings case in *American Sphinx* when he reached the point in Jefferson's life when Callender made the charge, and included a brief appendix on the case:

> . . . [T]he most sensational accusation made against Jefferson, a charge of sexual (and in its own day racial) impropriety that became the equivalent of a tin can tied to Jefferson's reputation that has continued to rattle through the ages and the pages of the history books. . . . It has been a publicist's dream ever since, because the charges cannot be conclusively proved or disproved and because advocates on each side of the debate have just enough evidence at their disposal to block a comfortable verdict for the opposition. (1997, 216–17)

In "the early nineteenth century . . . Callender published his charges":

> . . . the middle decades of the nineteenth century produced two new pieces of evidence, each important in its own right, but together contradicting each other. In 1873 Madison Hemings, Sally's next to last child (born in 1805) gave an interview to the *Pike County* (Ohio) *Republican* claiming that his mother had identified Thomas Jefferson as his father and, in fact, the father of all her five children. This claim was verified by Israel Jefferson, another ex-slave from Monticello, also living in Ohio at the time and a longtime friend of Madison Hemings'. The following year, in 1874, James Parton published his *Life of Thomas Jefferson* [1971] and reported another story that had been circulating with the Jefferson and Randolph families for many years— to wit, that Jefferson's nephew Peter Carr had been the father of all or most of Sally's children. . . . This version of miscegenation on the mountaintop received partial corroboration from Edmund Bacon, the former manager of Monticello, who claimed in his interview of 1862 that he had seen another man leaving Sally's quarters "many a morning." There were now two different versions of the Sally story placed before the public, one rooted in the oral tradition of the Hemings family and the other in the oral tradition of the white descendants of the Jefferson–Randolph family. (1997, 304)

## Discussion: Evidence, reasoning, and the biographers

We suggest asking two questions about the excerpts just presented. How seriously do they take the testimony provided by Madison Hemings? What is the nature of the case they make for rejecting the testimony? Merrill Peterson, the author of the first excerpt, provides us with the most striking contrast in the answers to our two questions. He took Madison Hemings' memoir seriously, noting its vivid tone, and stressing its accuracy about Jefferson as a person and about life at Monticello. Yet in the next sentence, Peterson dismisses the memoir as not proof of anything at all. The implicit reason appears to be that Madison Hemings grew up at Monticello so of course he can be vivid and accurate about life there, but his claim to Jefferson as a father need not be considered since it is just one more "Negroes' pathetic wish for a little pride." The story was revived, according to Peterson, because of the abolitionists' desire to attack slavery, not because of evidence that requires serious consideration. While he writes from the assumption that it would be a source of pride for a slave to claim descent from Thomas Jefferson, he does not write about the possible family pride that could have motivated Bacon or Jefferson's grandchildren to deny the rumor. We read Peterson's dismissive tone toward Madison Hemings, and his reasons for not considering the charge, as the products of racial bias in his viewpoint, preventing him from taking Madison Hemings' claim seriously. How did you read this section? How would your students evaluate it?

Dumas Malone accepted that Jefferson had treated the Hemings family with exceptional care, and suggested Jefferson acted this way because Sally Hemings and her brothers and sisters were the half-siblings of his wife, Martha Wayles Jefferson. As we mentioned in the previous chapter, Elizabeth (Betty) Hemings was said to have been the companion of John Wayles after his wife died, and that he had a number of children with her. John Wayles was Martha Wayles Jefferson's father. In effect, according to Malone, Jefferson acknowledged his half-sister and brother-in-laws. Malone's explanation recognized that Jefferson could acknowledge a degree of kinship with his slaves. Gordon-Reed (1997) points out that this is not exactly the case. None of Elizabeth Hemings' other grandchildren were set free—it was only the family of her daughter Sally who all escaped slavery.

Malone confronted the evidence showing special treatment of Sally Hemings and her family, but to us it appears that his response shows he was incapable of weighing all of the evidence and answered with a misleading half-truth. The truth is that oral tradition does claim the relationship between Elizabeth Hemings and John Wayles, making Sally and her siblings the half-brothers and half-sisters of Martha Jefferson. The falsehood is that any special treatment that Jefferson extended for that reason would have applied to many more families on the plantation. Perhaps Malone's own biases caused him to unconsciously avoid the degree of special treatment Jefferson extended to Sally Hemings; of everyone at Monticello only her children were all freed.

Malone's other writing on the case does not require such careful consideration. He does not explain what *errors* were present in Madison Hemings' memoir, or why they are crucial. Conceding that Madison Hemings might have reported his mother's story accurately, Malone also suggests, without citing evidence, that Sally Hemings might have been motivated to make that claim by "vanity." As we read Malone's words, he makes no effort to understand Sally Hemings in her own terms, and certainly does not credit her with the feelings of affection or responsibility we would ordinarily presume a woman has toward the father of her children. The presumption that Sally Hemings would have lied to her son about the identity of his father out of "vanity" fails to think seriously about her motherhood. In contrast, Malone did credit Jefferson with feelings of responsibility toward the slave family of his dead wife. In the absence of some specific reason to think otherwise, it appears to us that Malone demonstrated a racial bias against Sally Hemings and her family when he speculated beyond the strict limits of his evidence. Finally, he quickly moved from the memoir to the evidence against the liaison without a significant discussion of any merits the memoir might have possessed. His attitude toward significant testimony from the enslaved, or African American side of the family, seems dismissive.

Joseph Ellis, the last major biographer to write about Jefferson before the DNA studies emerged, took a far different line from his predecessors, yet his words bear some striking similarities. Unlike Peterson or Malone, he stated at the beginning of his book, in the middle, and at the end, that "the truly defining truth about the Sally Hemings story is that we will never know. . . . This is one mystery that is destined to remain unsolved" (1998, 21). In the preceding selection, Ellis takes care not to privilege one reading of the evidence over the other.

When choosing where in his biography to discuss the relationship, Ellis made the same decision Malone made thirty years before. Ellis introduced the discussion of a relationship between Thomas Jefferson and Sally Hemings into his text at the moment in Jefferson's first term as President of the United States when Callender made the charge public. Ellis did not write about the relationship as part of his sketch of Jefferson's psychology; he wrote about it as a political obstacle Jefferson faced. Despite having stated that there was sufficient reason to decide either way, as a biographer Ellis effectively discounted the possibility of an affair when sketching his portrait of Jefferson. On the one hand, Ellis made a judgment about the affair as a scholar and biographer, and stuck with it, while conceding that the opposite judgment could be correct. These decisions are a far cry from the overt racism in the writing of Peterson or Malone. On the other hand, Ellis chose not to speculate at all about Jefferson's inner life on the chance that the African American oral tradition, and related evidence, was true. In such a contested case, with the outcome meaning a quite different view of Jefferson as a person, choosing not to write at all about Jefferson as if he were involved in a relationship with Sally Hemings expresses a subtle bias against one reading of the evidence.

Calling a conscious scholarly choice *biased* may seem too strong, yet we stand by the term. We should also note that Ellis was the coauthor on the paper in *Nature* that argued, based on the DNA findings, that the weight of evidence now supported the claim that Jefferson was the father of one and likely all of Sally Hemings' children (Lander and Ellis, 1998). Whatever bias we detect in his treatment of Jefferson in the biography, *American Sphinx*, did not prevent him from changing his mind in the face of new evidence.

Ellis, like Malone, included an appendix in which he described the evidence in the Jefferson/Hemings case and expressed his own judgment. Unlike Malone, he emphasized that the evidence could be read either way, and unlike Peterson he stuck to the evidence, not allegations about the abolitionists conspiring against slavery by attacking Thomas Jefferson. The section quoted before provides Ellis' assessment of Madison Hemings' memoir and the related evidence we examined in Chapter 4. He noted that Madison Hemings' version of the past had been corroborated by Israel Jefferson. Ellis wrote that at the same time a competing oral tradition developed with the white descendants of Monticello, in the Jefferson biography published by James Parton. That book contained the tradition that Thomas Jefferson Randolph had investigated and his rebuttal of the possibility that his grandfather had been the parent of Sally Hemings' children, saying that it had been Peter Carr. This itself is problematic because it is a mistaken citation. On page 569 of Parton's biography (1971 Da Capo Press edition), he wrote: "The father of those children was a near relation of the Jeffersons, who need not be named." We are not certain that the Ellis mistake demonstrates anything beyond the difficulty of maintaining total accuracy in the face of so many details, but it underscores the possibility that an historian is also prone to errors. (We are aware that our book may contain similar errors, despite our best efforts and help from generous scholars.) Ellis' mistake reminds us that we need to respect a biographers' work while still making critical judgments, and even double-check an historian's portrayal of *the facts*.

Ellis also cites Bacon's account as a partial corroboration of this Carr story. Two oral traditions exist side by side, without reason to choose one over the other. You have examined the evidence in the previous chapter, and aside from the DNA evidence, there was nothing you saw that Ellis did not see. Does his depiction of the evidence seem fair? Is it a case of two equally plausible oral traditions? Is the testimony of Madison Hemings, who grew up at Monticello with Sally Hemings and Thomas Jefferson around, only equal in weight to the testimony of Thomas Jefferson's grandson as reported to a biographer? Is Edmund Bacon's complete story, including the account of his role in the "escape" of Harriet Hemings, really even a partial confirmation of the Carr story, particularly since Pierson did not print a name of the person-who-was-not-Jefferson whom he saw emerge from Sally Hemings' bedroom? In his appendix, Ellis did not discuss the other issue—Jefferson's direct involvement in freeing all of Sally Hemings' children—raised by Bacon's testimony. Is this an example of bias? Is it racial bias because it equates perhaps less-direct testimony by white relatives to more-direct testimony by black relatives? Is it the bias of a reverence for Jefferson, or an inertia based on one scholarly status quo?

The value in considering the possibility of bias in the writing of Joseph Ellis is that it is not simple to locate, not an overt racism like that expressed by Peterson or Malone. Ellis was quick to equate both family traditions without weighing them closely, one against the other, and he only examined the consequences of one conclusion about Jefferson while saying that both were possible. Considering Ellis forces us to think about ourselves, and to wonder about our own capacity for clear thinking when faced with the icons of the American nation, or of the democratic tradition. Even when we say the evidence is inconclusive, do we truly consider both sides? We can reexamine this question immediately, as we leave the question of how the historians treated Madison Hemings' testimony and the specific evidence, and move toward a more abstract ground—their writing about the character of Thomas Jefferson.

The bottom line, for Malone and Ellis, in dismissing the charges that Thomas Jefferson and Sally Hemings had a long, intimate relationship, and that Thomas Jefferson fathered her children, was that it was out of character for Thomas Jefferson to have had such a relationship. Next, we present selections from their writings about the character issue, and then comment on them.

## MALONE ON JEFFERSON'S *CHARACTER*

They [the behaviors charged] were distinctly out of character, being virtually unthinkable in a man of Jefferson's moral standards and habitual conduct. To say this is not to claim that he was a plaster saint and incapable of moral lapses. But his major weaknesses were not of this sort; and while he might have occasionally fallen from grace, as so many men have done so often, it is virtually inconceivable that this fastidious gentleman whose devotion to his dead wife's memory and to the happiness of his daughters and grandchildren bordered on the excessive could have carried on through a period of years a vulgar liaison which his own family could not have failed to detect. It would be as absurd as to charge this consistently temperate man with being, through a long period, a secret drunkard. (1970, 214)

The miscegenation story, as elaborated after Jefferson's death, assigned to him the paternity of the children borne by Sally Hemings during his presidency, two of them in his second term . . . [Anyone who believed this story] assumed that, despite the publicity Callender and the Federalist newspapers gave his alleged liaison, he continued it during his sixties while holding the highest office in the land, thus defying public opinion and wholly disregarding the feelings of his beloved daughters and grandchildren. To charge him with that degree of imprudence and insensitivity requires extraordinary credulity. (1970, 494)

## ELLIS ON JEFFERSON'S *CHARACTER*

. . . [A] long-term sexual relationship with one of his slaves was not in character for Jefferson, who spent much of his adult life creating distances between his personal perceptions and the palpable reality of slavery and who consistently fled from intimacy in favor of highly idealized and sentimentalized versions of affection. (1998, 219)

. . . [F]or those who demand an answer the only recourse is plausible conjecture. . . . In that spirit, which we might call the spirit of responsible speculation, after five years of mulling over the huge cache of evidence that does exist on the thought and character of the historical Jefferson, I have concluded that the likelihood of a liaison with Sally Hemings is remote. . . .

Sally's last two children, Madison and Easton, were born after Callender's charges created the public scandal in 1802, and it is difficult to believe that Jefferson would have persisted in producing progeny with Sally once the secret had been exposed and the Federalist press was poised to report it.

. . . [W]hat my own immersion in the historical evidence has led me to conclude as well, is that for most of his adult life he lacked the capacity for the direct and physical expression of his sexual energies. Henry Adams put it most explicitly when he said that Jefferson's temperament was "almost feminine." When scholarly defenders like Dumas Malone and Merrill Peterson claimed that Jefferson was "not the kind of man" to engage in illicit sex with an attractive mulatto slave, they were right for reasons that went deeper than matters of male gallantry and aristocratic honor. Jefferson consummated his relationships with women at a more rarefied level, where the palpable realities of physical intimacy were routinely sublimated to safer and more sentimental regions. He made a point of insulating himself from direct exposure to the unmitigated meaning of both sex and slavery, a lifelong tendency that an enduring liaison with Sally Hemings would have violated in ways he found intolerable . . . his urge to remain oblivious was considerably stronger than his sexual drive . . . nothing we know about Jefferson supports the linkage between sex and sensuality. His most sensual statements were aimed at beautiful buildings rather than beautiful women. In sum, the alleged relationship with Sally Hemings, if it did exist, defied the dominant patterns of his personality. (1998, 305–306)

## Discussion: The character of Thomas Jefferson

It is hard to read the selection written by Dumas Malone who could not believe that Jefferson would have carried on a "vulgar" liaison with Sally Hemings because it would have marred the happiness of his children and sullied the office of President of the United States. If anyone is entitled to speculate on Jefferson's character, it is Malone who dedicated his lifetime to studying Jefferson; yet, on this point, Malone recorded incredulity and racial prejudice rather than historical reasoning. This is the language of a character witness for the defense during a trial! Annette Gordon-Reed points out another flaw in this assessment of Jefferson's character. The evidence of Jefferson's life suggests that he did not always sacrifice his desires to protect his children's happiness. Most glaringly, Jefferson persisted in hosting many people and events at Monticello, and in purchasing the most expensive wines, long after he entered into financial difficulties. Driving himself into financial ruin, he was unable to make long-term provisions for the financial well-being of his beloved daughters (Gordon-Reed 1997). Malone's argument from *character* reads as an argument from a fixed belief that Thomas Jefferson would not have slept with a slave.

Ellis' writing lacks Malone's explicit racial overtones. He echoed Malone's thinking on the first point, that Jefferson would not have continued the relationship with Hemings even after Callender published his charges. In agreeing, Ellis did not write about public opinion or the high office of President, but muted the point to a consideration of political strategy, that it would have been so unwise to provide fuel for his enemies that Jefferson would not have continued to see Sally Hemings. Since Hemings continued to have children, the father could not have been Thomas Jefferson.

Ellis makes two other points in this selection. First, that Jefferson avoided the contradictions of slave ownership and a twenty-eight-year-long sexual relationship with a slave would have overtaxed even his capacity for self-deception. Second, that Jefferson sublimated his sex drive and directed it at buildings not women. These are both interpretations Ellis arrived at after five years of studying Jefferson's thoughts by perusing all of the documents he could find. Reading these words after the DNA tests, we are struck by how vulnerable all of our interpretations are to revision in the face of new evidence, or new ways of thinking. Even when new evidence is unlikely to appear, we ought to regard all *conclusions* in history as best guesses. We should be even more cautious when we are explaining something as diffuse as a person's character, and not a particular action. Apparently, Jefferson had a greater capacity for self-deception than Joseph Ellis imagined.

As for Thomas Jefferson's sex drive, we would like to contrast the interpretation Ellis provided in 1998 with a quite different perspective from another historian who wrote in 1988. Jack McLaughlin's book, *Jefferson and Monticello*, is a wonderful source for anyone interested in thinking about the day-to-day aspects of life at Monticello, and what life on that mountaintop reveals about Jefferson. Too, he shares with Ellis the notion that Jefferson was infatuated with buildings. McLaughlin writes that he produced the book "to tell about Jefferson's love affair with a house, and the remarkably difficult time he had consummating it" (1988, viii). Looking at the same evidence, but emphasizing a different aspect of it, McLaughlin came up with a dramatically different understanding of Jefferson's sexual desires. Note his contrasting interpretation of the same evidence:

> Whatever Jefferson's sexual proclivities may have been, his marriage demonstrates that he was very much a sexual creature. In ten years, he fathered six children, several of them at times when Martha's health should have precluded pregnancy. But Jefferson was as unwilling as any male of his class to deny himself the pleasures of the marital bed because of his wife's poor health. And Jefferson, who was as knowledgeable about health and medicine as any layman of his age, appears to have made no attempt to practice contraception or child planning . . . Martha Jefferson's terminal illness . . . was a lingering one, following a pregnancy. (1988, 196)

> The extremity of Jefferson's grief [over his wife's death] circulated among his friends and caused some concern. . . . The two most common dynamic emotions in cases of violent bereavement are guilt and anger. . . . [H]er death was ultimately caused, not by Martha's weakness of will or lack of determination to survive, but by the pregnancies resulting from the sexual demands of her husband. Jefferson could not help but face this conclusion and hold himself responsible for his wife's death. Throughout his life he had practiced a stoic control over his passions, but the liberties of the marriage bed were a temptation he was unwilling or unable to check—even though he knew the inevitable pregnancies placed her seriously at risk. (1988, 200–201)

Ellis, writing about the same death, concluded: "Jefferson did not seem to possess any sense of complicity in causing her pregnancies or any sense of warning as her health deteriorated after each new miscarriage or birth" (1998, 67). He reached the opposite interpretation about the same event. This is another case where the truth does not lie in the *middle* but where historians have gone beyond recounting events and behaviors and have sought to understand Jefferson's internal life. Making informed judgments about the reasons why people act is at the core of historians' work, it is where recording gives way to understanding and empathy. It is also treacherous. Ellis concluded that after Martha Wayles Jefferson's death, Thomas Jefferson decided never to allow himself to become vulnerable to such pain again, and sublimated his sex drive, never strong to begin with, in other parts of his life, particularly his building projects. The DNA evidence argues that

McLaughlin's emphasis on Jefferson's strong sex drive was closer to the truth, and that within a few years Jefferson embarked on another sexual relationship that led to a second family.

Writing about character is necessary. After a six-volume life history, or even a single-volume biography, we want the benefit of the biographer's judgments about the person at the center of the story. We should also be wary of those judgments, knowing that too much time with a single person may let us know them well but may also blind an historian to parts of someone's personality. The specific case of Jefferson and Hemings leads us to another conclusion. Broad generalizations about a person's character are fine, but they should not be weighed more heavily than specific historical evidence. Malone and Ellis allowed their perceptions of Jefferson's character to outweigh specific evidence.

## Reflections on the historical writing about Jefferson and Hemings as a mystery

What do students gain when we line up excerpts from the writings about the Jefferson/Hemings case and have them examine selections from various authors in the same fashion that they examine the evidence in the case itself? We hope that the students gain confidence in their ability to interpret evidence, an appreciation for viewpoint in historical writing, and see that the most compelling questions in history are open for their (re)consideration. In the selections in the Mystery Packets, the historians deal with evidence that the students have investigated themselves in the previous chapter. After reading the Madison Hemings memoir, the Israel Jefferson memoir, the Edmund Bacon testimony, understanding Thomas Jefferson's Will, and reaching their own conclusions about the meaning of that evidence, our students are able to evaluate how Peterson, Malone, and Ellis read those sources. We hope that as students read the excerpts from the historians they will discover that, having read the key sources described by these Jefferson scholars, they were able to learn enough in our classrooms to draw valid conclusions about the Jefferson/Hemings case.

We also expect that students will see the importance of the historians' viewpoints in approaching the sources. Peterson and Malone could not quite conceive of "Negroes" as equals, or understand anything other than that former slaves claiming descent from Thomas Jefferson were reaching for dignity. Ellis provides students with a different take on viewpoint. Despite proclaiming that the evidence was equally strong on either side of the case, Ellis wrote his biography only on the basis of Jefferson not having a sexual relationship with Sally Hemings, thus expressing a different sort of bias. Perhaps this is the bias of the status quo, of the belief by most Jefferson biographers that he was not the father of Sally Hemings' children. Perhaps there was an element of racial bias lurking deep in the background, the kind of unconscious bias that might make it difficult for a white American to conceive of Jefferson having a relationship with his slave. Students need to be aware of the influential role that viewpoint plays in all of the studies historians carry out.

Finally, the section on character might hold the most profound lesson about history writing. Many students conceive of history as a series of facts, and treat most research assignments as mining expeditions in which they extract the facts from historians' books and then line them up in order to form a paper. The section on character could liberate such students from an extractive approach to history. There was nothing *factual* about the sections on character. The evidence of Jefferson's conduct at many times in his life informed that writing, as did all of Jefferson's own writing. But the conclusions leapt beyond the evidence, to a realm of *responsible speculation* where historians attempt to bring the past alive. Students writing about Jefferson could cite Ellis and cite McLaughlin, but they would have to decide for themselves which view of Jefferson's sex drive best fits the evidence, and how they should apply that understanding to Jefferson and Hemings. Historical writing is always full of just such gaps in the record and leaps beyond the evidence. Those gaps give students much more control over their papers, and change their job as paper writers from miners extracting facts into minors making informed judgments about historical writing.

## The historical significance of Jefferson and Hemings

What is the significance of the Jefferson/Hemings case compared, perhaps, to his achievements in writing the Declaration of Independence, the Virginia and Kentucky Resolutions, or negotiating the Louisiana Purchase? We have made the case that this further investigation of the Jefferson/Hemings relationship takes us much further into issues of slavery, race, and daily life in eighteenth- and nineteenth-century America than the basic view of the case provided in Chapter 4. But why should we make time for this investigation of Jefferson when we might explore the mystery of his resolutions in the Declaration of Independence, including the draft's charge that the King forced slavery on the colonies? Or, if we do not dwell on the relationship with Sally Hemings, we might contrast Jefferson's commitment to limiting federal power when he was out of government to when he was President. These are the curricular choices every teacher faces.

One answer to the question is the excitement factor. Your students do need to know about the Louisiana Purchase, but they might pay more attention to the "sexy" Jefferson/Hemings case and therefore learn more. Perhaps what they need to know about it is relatively straightforward: when it happened, who was involved, and where exactly it is located; so you could fit the Louisiana Purchase in and leave time for an extended investigation of Jefferson and Hemings. Another answer might be one of purpose and planning. The Jefferson/Hemings case might provide a unique opportunity to study issues of plantation life, while the question of the relative power of the federal government can be encountered at many more points, from Andrew Jackson and South Carolina to the Civil War to World War I to the New Deal to the Reagan presidency. So, perhaps focusing on the Jefferson/Hemings case in a chronological course means that your students will not carefully study the question of federal-versus-state power, but simply have that idea briefly introduced. They will still encounter struggles over federal authority at other points in the course. A variation on this answer would ask, pragmatically: For what questions do you have the material that will allow your students to conduct an in-depth investigation? If you do not have sources for an extended study of the debates over the wording of the Declaration of Independence, that may be a reason to choose the Jefferson/Hemings case as the topic for an extended study; to familiarize your students with other ideas from the mind of the person who wrote the Declaration of Independence.

We want to suggest a different answer, one that more directly addresses the question of historical significance. What kind of history are we writing, and what is the basis from which we derive significance? Gerda Lerner, a past president of the Organization of American Historians, who launched a doctoral program in women's history at the University of Wisconsin, argues that we have constructed history "only in male-centered terms." In Chapter 2, when we gave the example of asking about the role of women in a strike, we risk leaving out how women contributed to the larger labor movement. A strike may have been a "male activity" at that time. Women were involved in the strike, but it may be that other actions by women did more to create a society that could accept labor unions than whatever they contributed to a strike.

Writing about women in the antislavery movement, Lerner suggests that looking at women's *contributions* to abolitionism might lead one to focus on abolitionist women whose demand to lecture in public split and weakened the abolitionist movement. Looking at their impact on nineteenth-century male activities, voting behavior, and politics, one would find minimal impact. But looking at women's role in and experience of abolitionism brings a different answer into focus. "Organization building, the spreading of literature, petitioning, participation in slave rescues—helped to create changes in the climate of opinion in the North and West that were essential to the growth of the political antislavery movement" (Lerner 1997, 120). Another way of saying this is that what women do and say is as important as what men do and say, and so we should ask "what were the women doing while the men were doing what we are teaching?" (Lerner 1997, 143). This would suggest that a history of childrearing is as important in shaping our lives as a history of trade agreements; that work outside the home is equally important as work inside the home. But this is not simply an additive strategy of teaching about "production and reproduction," it is teaching about "a world populated by male and female actors and evaluated by male *and* female standards" (Lerner 1997, 143).

Well, what does this have to do with Jefferson? This means that when we think about what shapes our lives, we make the case that our ideas of race, and the history of how we have handled our domestic life including questions of gender and sexuality, are as "shaping" of our lives as the Louisiana Purchase, and arguably more complex to study. The Louisiana Purchase may have reshaped the nation's boundaries so it is historically significant. But the boundaries Jefferson and Hemings and their children negotiated at Monticello, the boundaries between black and white, free and slave, male and female, have an equal or greater impact on "where we can go" with our lives. The DNA study on Hemings and Jefferson descendants itself "opened up new ways of looking at and thinking about a wide range of topics . . . [Historians] recognized as 'important'—from race relations to the history of sexuality, to the way we practice history. New ways of imagining the past and new areas of research seemed to open before us . . . we encountered uncharted terrrain: the social world that Jefferson and Hemings inhabited and, indeed, created" (Lewis and Onuf 1999, 4). Imagining, inhabiting, and exploring this world is, we argue, as historically significant as investigating any other aspect of Jefferson's life. The Declaration of Independence, the Virginia and Kentucky Resolutions, the Embargo, and the Louisiana Purchase all have important political ramifications, and yet we also live with the results of the world of race he and Hemings lived and shaped at Monticello.

The June 2002 Advanced Placement exam in United States History asked students to choose two out of three leaders—Washington, Adams, Jefferson—and analyze their contributions to the stability of the U.S. government after the adoption of the Constitution. Of the students who picked Jefferson, many wrote about the Louisiana Purchase. Fewer wrote about the Virginia and Kentucky Resolutions and their destabilizing contribution to Nullification and the use John Calhoun would make of the concept. Fewer still wrote about his silence on slavery and its destructive impact on the government. Studying Jefferson and Hemings might enable students to bring a broader perspective to bear on what makes a government stable, one that would incorporate the broader worlds Gerda Lerner urges us to consider.

Jefferson is also a powerful symbol for the study of race. Gordon Wood, a prominent historian of the American Revolution, asks: "What precisely is it we do, or are supposed to do, in writing about a heavily symbolic figure like Jefferson?" (1999, 32). Winthrop Jordan, reflecting on the DNA discoveries, remembered his early on race in America and how he devoted few pages to the relationship between Jefferson and Hemings, "I thought arrogantly that I had broader and more important things in mind" (1999, 50). In Jordan's reconsideration, he argues that the relationship between Jefferson and Sally Hemings provides many clues into the ideas Jefferson developed about boundaries between people and suggests that the divide between black and white is only one of many paired opposites that mattered to Jefferson. Rethinking Jefferson's ability to cross those boundaries and have a relationship with Sally Hemings, Jordan stresses Hemings' class position and accent, and revisits Jefferson's thinking about gender, along with her race and slavery. Jordan also suggests that historians ought to have paid attention to public interest in the Jefferson/Hemings relationship: "What is important historically about the Hemings-Jefferson affair is that it has seemed to so many Americans to have mattered" (1999, 50).

Part of what we do in classrooms is help students distinguish between what is interesting to them, a battle or an idea they like, and what we consider to be historically significant. Yet, perhaps, in this case of personal life, the public saw something about the importance of Jefferson's life that historians are now embracing. The interplay between an event and its significance is somewhat fluid and Jefferson and Hemings may be a touchstone for many Americans in sorting out their ideas of race. To illustrate that importance, we close with a section of oral history from Horace Harnet, a member of Mississippi's white supremacist White Citizen's Councils in the 1950s and 1960s and a former member of the Mississippi State Assembly. He spoke about his views on race (and less explicitly gender) with sociologist Jane Adams, and toward the end uses Jefferson as an example justifying one type of interracial liaison. This extended quotation illustrates our belief that studying the Jefferson/Hemings relationship for an understanding of the eighteenth and nineteenth centuries, and studying people's thinking about it now, is significant enough to justify extended investigation of it even at the cost of, for example, an extended look at the Louisiana Purchase or the Louis and Clark expedition.

*J*: What makes different races?

*H*: The Lord made them different.

*J*: Are Jews a different race?

*H*: No, they're not. They're a different religion.

*J*: Are Chinese a different race?

*H*: Oh, yeah.

*J*: Are Italians a different race?

*H*: Their culture's different. I don't say they're not a different race. They're not a different race. I think the Italians and the French and the Germans and the Russians too, all, white Americans, they're all the same race. But, of course, the blacks are a different race and the Indians are a different race and the Chinese are a different race and then you've got the Aborigines in Australia.

*J*: How do you distinguish one race from another?

*H*: Well, by their char . . . facial—physical characteristics is the main thing, their physical characteristics.

The good Good Lord charged the Jewish race to be pure and of course they didn't and he punished them [in Biblical times]. And He had his reasons and I don't question them. I believed in that, in racial purity. I surely did. And I still do.

We had one of the most prominent citizens in town here, he had a white family and he had some blacks on the side. And he took care of his blacks. He set his black son up in business on Main Street, right here.

I'm not going to say it was accepted but it was practiced that, there might be a high yellow black woman in the yard. She might be the cook. Of course, they're blaming Thomas Jefferson with some of that. And actually, that may be true. And he's the only President I have any direct relation to. Collaterally, we have some of the same genes. And he's one of my favorite American heroes, Thomas Jefferson. And if he, after his wife died, if he cohabited with an attractive black female there, why you know that, that was winked at.

We reprint this conversation here for easy reference; you can find it, and more of the work Jane Adams has done on this subject, at her website, *www.siu.edu /~anthro/adams*. The Adams interview with Harnet demonstrates that the relationship between Thomas Jefferson and Sally Hemings shapes the way people think about race in this country. We rarely hear the voices of segregationists, but here is one person grappling with his own racial code, and the evidence of its violation. This is a striking conversation in its own right, but students have a much more in-depth ability to wrestle with Horace Harnet if they have struggled with Thomas Jefferson. Aside from condemning racism, they will have had some experience studying someone who lived day by day with fixed racial categories and in a community that crossed them. It is a *live* issue and, perhaps, will have more application for students, more significance (we are not making an argument about interest at the moment) than the Louisiana Purchase.

In May 2002 the Monticello Association, descendants of Jefferson through his children with Martha Wayles Jefferson, voted to keep the descendants of Sally Hemings out of the Jefferson family plot at Monticello. This decision, reported in national papers (*New York Times*, 6 June 2002) and in local papers, *Long Island Newsday*, is one example of the continuing struggle over racial definitions and *boundaries*. If you like, we can call this study a different kind of geography than the Louisiana Purchase, a *human* geography, which in our view is just as important as lines drawn on a map.

## Suggested activities: Teaching about the public and private lives of famous people

In this chapter we have concentrated on the topic of Thomas Jefferson's relationship to Sally Hemings. We have discussed the proof of Jefferson's paternity of both a white and a black family who are still with us, forming part of present-day American society. While this case study concentrates on one or two families, depending on how you want to count or recognize the Jefferson branches, you may want to use this set of evidence as a model for a variety of other investigations. You could focus on issues of character; on questions of public and private behavior; on problems of biography and autobiography; and/or on historians' susceptibility, just like the rest of us, to social pressures in which the atmosphere may condone silence or promote media attack. Here are some suggestions for possible follow-up activities and studies to use instead of or in addition to the Jefferson/Hemings case.

1. View one or more episodes of the once-popular British TV series *Upstairs/ Downstairs* and compare the lives of the upper class and the servant class. Consider these relationships in light of the Jefferson/Hemings case and discuss whether it is possible for historians to easily bring to light class, race, and gender relationships when social lines are crossed.

2. Investigate the romances of President John F. Kennedy while he was in office, and the media and historical view of his private life in succeeding decades. Why do you think so little attention was paid to his private life when he was President, while so much more attention focused on his affairs later on? Was his life similar to or different from Jefferson's?

3. Choose any two, three, or four famous men or women, particularly political leaders, and read at least two brief or full biographies on their public and private lives, depending on how much time you want to devote to this. Focus on how easy or difficult it is to obtain information about their private lives as compared with their public records.

4. Investigate the private life of Mrs. Eleanor and President Franklin Delano Roosevelt. Were their private relationships kept secret at the time of his presidency? Was there media and public criticism of the President's personal life while he was in office, or did this only appear afterward?

5. Continue the Jefferson/Hemings case by collecting studies of master–slave relationships. Were liaisons between masters and their female slaves accepted at the time by society? Were slaves generally treated better or worse than Sally Hemings? Is it easy or difficult to find evidence of private lives, particularly sexual behavior, in the late eighteenth and early nineteenth centuries?

6. Take a look at the case of President Bill Clinton, and his much-talked-about affair with Monica Lewinsky: Is this much like or very unlike Jefferson's paternity mystery? Was it a mystery at all; if so, what is the mystery? Why has society examined every personal and private relationship in the case of Bill Clinton, but overlooked or suppressed so much for other Presidents?

7. Set up an Ethical Court in your classroom and ask students to review the evidence of Jefferson's personal life and his attitudes toward slaves as compared to his official writings about life, liberty, and freedom. Ask students to serve as Value Guardians, providing roles for judges, jury members, and attorneys. Place Thomas Jefferson on trial for hypocrisy and double-dealing: How does the Ethical Court see his case and what verdict would they turn in for him: guilty or innocent, or extenuating circumstances due to the times he lived in? By the way, just because people did things in the past that we now regard as wrong, was it excusable then?

8. Call on students to write letters in the manner of the times as though they were Jefferson, Hemings, or one or more of his offspring defending or explaining the relationship. Call on other students to rewrite the work of the historians who were quoted (or one they researched on their own), correcting any mistakes they see and adjusting her or his viewpoint to be as honest and as true to the evidence as possible.

    For example, a romantic Hemings letter might say:

    > I really loved Tom, but how could we be married? It was an impossible love and I knew it. After all, Tom was the Master and had already been married. But I knew he loved me best, and took care of my children as best he could

without being noticed by the daughters of the House. He also took care of their family as well, and all of us tried very hard not to notice each other.

For example, an unromantic Jefferson letter might say:

Keep your nose out of my business. My love life is my own, and not of any interest to you. I keep public and private business strictly separate, you know, and this has nothing to do with my role as President.

What do you think you would say in your letter?

## Conclusion: Opening new mysteries by solving old mysteries

In this chapter, we continued our investigation of the mystery of Jefferson's relationship with Sally Hemings, but we added a new wrinkle to our inquiry in the form of commentary from historians. You may feel that the mystery of a secret, or not so secret, love affair between Thomas Jefferson and his slave has been amply solved. Maybe you are quite right, but we would like to convince you that many more mysteries have been opened up in the process.

First, we still have a mystery of motivation and viewpoint. Was Jefferson really in love with Sally? Are there any indications of love? Were her children treated better than the average slave in his household? Did Jefferson simply take advantage of the situation, much like other masters of his time did, and think little of it? What motivations and feelings might you attribute to Jefferson based on our evidence? Given the kind of person he was—intellectual, serious, considerate— how would his ideas square with or contradict his private behavior?

Second, we have a mystery of social context and corroboration. Since his enemies criticized Jefferson at the time for a suspected liaison, why didn't that seem to take hold in the Virginia community? Why didn't the attacks on him seem to cause him political problems in Washington when he was President? Weren't there already several reports and criticisms available that supported, corroborated, the idea that Jefferson was involved with a female slave? Private life may be invaded by public scrutiny when people feel that a person's behavior has impacted that part of their performance that affects us all, perhaps. Several recent Presidents, for example, have had a lot more trouble than Jefferson for what many would say were a lot less sin. In terms of private peccadilloes and marital problems, Jefferson's actions might be viewed as a much more serious ethical problem than those of many other Presidents, if we want to develop this type of a comparison. Why have some recent Presidents been more reviled, attacked, and excoriated by the press, media, and the community for their wrongdoing than Jefferson? What sort of social context, temper of the times, causes people to focus on the private life of Presidents and other leaders, while ignoring their behavior at other times?

Third, we have a mystery of scholarship. Historians, professionals in the art and science of studying the past, are supposed to be detective-like and critical-minded in their pursuit of *Truth*. Might we suggest, as you have undoubtedly already concluded from the historians we have quoted, that these scholars are often just as subject to community values as us ordinary human beings. They may overlook, forgive, or studiously avoid (pun) difficult and damaging evidence about famous figures, great leaders, and such, so much so that they purposely, perhaps, or subconsciously, perhaps, suppress evidence. Why? Maybe the historian doesn't want to face up to the truth? Maybe he or she cannot bring himself or herself to believe that someone heroic or outstanding has feet of clay, faults, and lustful yearnings? Perhaps historians see themselves as preservers of an historical figure's *image*? It is often difficult, if not impossible, to tease motives out of historians, particularly those who are trying to claim objectivity and write in a matter-of-fact style. Maybe it would be a lot better if historians laid their prejudices and assumptions out for us mortals so that we can get a better fix on their values and theories, applying these to their writings, thereby being able to adjust for personal preferences and viewpoints.

Fourth, we have a mystery of public and private life in American history. It seems that on some occasions, the public is deeply interested in the private lives of leaders and famous people, while at other times they seem barely aware of these matters. Often, the media of the time—newspapers, television, films, journals, and so forth—fan the flames of interest with lurid stories of private scandal and corruption with great effect on the public. New laws are sometimes born as a result. Presidents have impeachment proceedings developed against them. People lose their jobs and/or much more. At other times, the media attacks vigorously and promotes social criticism and change, but the public seems dispirited or disinterested, so nothing much happens to the wrongdoers or to the system of public values. Private life remains private and all, or almost all, is forgotten. We might raise questions about the public's view of private life: When does private life really matter and when is it focused on the leadership of a country? On its elite? When is interest focused on the private life of entertainment figures and media stars? Why do certain periods of history, and some people, seem to provoke political conflict and attention in both public and private spheres of life? Conversely, what conditions and causes work to inhibit or control investigations and nosiness into private matters?

As a result of your study of Jefferson and Hemings, and of the historians who wrote about them, might you consider new theories of public interest in private life? On the one hand, inquiry into private relationships may tend to occur when the affairs affect lawmaking or the public behavior of leaders. On the other hand, perhaps not much attention is paid to those leaders who keep private matters tightly under control—out of sight from the public. In Jefferson's case, it could be that the general view of him as a great founding father of the United States worked to his benefit in keeping citizens and scholars out of his private life because few were especially interested in tarnishing his image. Since the Civil Rights Movement of the 1960s, we may have established more open, honest communications about race than in our past, so it seems legitimate to admit and discuss Jefferson's two families, the white and the black, together.

Perhaps we are in the process of forming an entirely new culture of publicity in which private life is not sacred anymore for anyone in the news. All noted people, in this new culture, are grist for the mill of media attention for an audience hungry for gossip and scandal, however embarrassing, or maybe exactly because it is so embarrassing. The new culture may enjoy reducing the great to the average, making us all one happy and nosy democratic family! But, again, maybe we need to review our understanding of American history, seek out past examples of inquiry into private lives, and compare how the publicity and scandals were handled. Our evidence may show that Americans have frequently been interested in private gossip and scandal, and that the frequency may depend on how much "good" stuff is available to the media of the time, or on how happy or unhappy people are with the economy and body politic of their day. What do you think?

# Resources

ELLIS, JOSEPH. 1997. *American Sphinx*. New York: Alfred A. Knopf.

FERGUSON, WILLIAM S. 1962. *The Practical Cogitator*. Boston: Houghton Mifflin.

FRENCH, SCOT A., AND EDWARD L. AYERS. 1993. "The Strange Career of Thomas Jefferson: Race and Slavery in American Memory, 1943–1993." In *Jeffersonian Legacies*, Peter S. Onuf, ed. Charlottesville, VA: University Press of Virginia.

GORDON-REED, ANNETTE. 1997. *Thomas Jefferson and Sally Hemings: An American Controversy*. Charlottesville, VA/London: University Press of Virginia.

JORDAN, WINTHROP. 1968. *White over Black: American Attitudes Toward the Negro 1550–1812*. Baltimore: Penguin Books.

JORDAN, WINTHROP. 1999. "Hemings and Jefferson: Redux" in *Sally Hemings and Thomas Jefferson: History, Memory, and Civic Culture*, Jan Lewis and Peter Onuf, eds. Charlottesville, VA/London: University Press of Virginia.

LERNER, GERDA. 1997. *Why History Matters*. New York: Oxford University Press.

LEWIS, JAN, AND PETER ONUF, eds. 1999. *Sally Hemings and Thomas Jefferson: History, Memory, and Civic Culture*. Charlottesville, VA/London: University Press of Virginia.

MALONE, DUMAS. 1970. *Jefferson the President, First Term*. Boston: Little, Brown.

MCLAUGHLIN, JACK. 1988. *Jefferson and Monticello*. New York: Henry Holt.

MORGAN, PHILLIP. 1999. "Interracial Sex in the Chesapeake." In Jan Lewis and Peter Onuf, eds., *Sally Hemmings and Thomas Jefferson: History, Memory, and Civic Culture*, Charlottesville, VA/London: University Press of Virginia.

*NEW YORK TIMES*. 2002. "Jefferson Group Bars Slave's Descendants." 6 June.

PARTON, JAMES. 1874, 1971 reprint. *Life of Thomas Jefferson*. New York: Da Capo Press.

PETERSON, MERRILL. 1960. *The Jefferson Image in the American Mind*. New York: Oxford University Press.

STANTON, LUCIA C. 1996. *Slavery at Monticello*. Monticello, VA: Thomas Jefferson Foundation.

STANTON, LUCIA C. 2000. *Free Some Day: The African American Families at Monticello.* Monticello, VA: Thomas Jefferson Foundation.

WOOD, GORDON, 1999. "The Ghosts of Monticello." In *Sally Hemings and Thomas Jefferson: History, Memory, and Civic Culture*, Jan Lewis and Peter Onuf, eds. Charlottesville, VA/London: University Press of Virginia.

# 6

# Conclusion
## Teaching History as Mystery

Charles Beard (1874–1948), a noteworthy American historian, was asked to sum up the lessons of history and make it brief. He responded by saying he could add it all up in four (we would say *mysterious*) sentences:

1. Whom the gods would destroy, they first make mad with power.
2. The mills of God grind slowly, but they grind exceedingly small.
3. The bee fertilizes the flower it robs.
4. When it is dark enough, you can see the stars.

## *David and Jack duke it out:* Act I

*Jack*: Minor mysteries are easy, really all about who, what, when, where, how, etc., trying to find a motive and a weapon like a game of *Clue*. A major mystery, by contrast, I think, has to contain value issues, as I call them. You think this is an *old-fashioned* term, but I still like it. I might be willing to call it ethical or philosophical issues if you like, or maybe theory but these issues have to, must include emotional problems, like the ones we raised about bias or prejudice in the historians' treatment of Thomas Jefferson and Sally Hemings.

*David*: I'll argue the point in a moment, but what are your criteria for linking a *value* with a major mystery?

*Jack*: Well, a deep and major mystery must have buried within it ethical questions that have persisted for hundreds of years. We might believe they are *solved* for now, but all of a sudden they pop up right over again.

*David*: So how about an example or two?

*Jack*: Well, ethical questions can be posed in almost any area but are supported by the kind of evidence a teacher provides to her or his students. If you provide disturbing evidence, controversial evidence, the ethical problems will rise right to the surface. You as a teacher will hardly have to do anything to get feedback. For example, we presented the eight-item mystery of Jefferson's two families as a *medium* mystery, and I agree with that assessment. When we expanded it to ask why the historians did not recognize the relationship until after the DNA testing (or if we had asked why even today the white half of the family fails to recognize the black half of the family), we make it a major mystery because of the value issues involved.

*David*: You mean that what we claimed in those chapters, that we are talking about race prejudice and that this is still with us in certain forms, is the *values* issue and that you want to use Jefferson's family as a way of leading into this problem?

*Jack*: Right, and it is a pretty knotty and pretty nasty problem. It is a problem of *them* and *us*, defining people as different because of their skin color, origins, or language. We actually don't allow such behaviors by law in many places but still follow by social custom, social custom that is a hangover from some of what I think are *bad old days* in American history. These are questions of bias built into the historical record.

*David*: You have said enough to clarify your idea, and I want to offer a counter-argument. I am not entirely comfortable with the *value* issues concept as necessary to make something a major mystery, or as necessarily missing from a minor mystery. An historical problem can have complex interpretative problems without raising complicated ethical issues. An example might be controversy over the origins of slavery in America. The records from the seventeenth-century are sparse, and we have to make informed judgments on the material we do have, guessing about the meaning residing in the original sources about the distinctions between slavery and indentured servitude. Moreover, we have a number of complicated concepts that may be elaborated by these documents (i.e., the Atlantic world, demands for labor, relative vulnerability of different populations, race as a social construction) and a theoretical debate over whether slavery created race, or if racial prejudice gave rise to slavery. This is a major mystery, but does not contain the same value issues that we confronted with Jefferson and how to judge him, or the subtle issues of bias that may exist in historians' accounts of Jefferson's relationship with Hemings. Enslavement, racial or otherwise, is wrong. Here is historical complexity without moral ambiguity.

*Jack*: You are hair splitting! If slavery or the meaning of race does not raise all sorts of ethical issues in the classroom, what does? And in our society because racism is still alive and well, and we do not all agree what is a racist statement or not, simply talking about race raises value problems. You cannot tell me that students will simply read the documents for what they can learn about the past, and not worry about how they speak about race that will influence the way their classmates or teachers judge them. It is that level of ethical charge that makes a major mystery.

*David*: Now you are the one making a statement so extreme as to be absurd. Sexuality is as charged as race, if not in our society than certainly in our schools. Yet we both know that a biology lesson on reproduction can be full of lists, that students can study complex evolutionary questions and confront major mysteries in biology and the sexual charge is not a part of it.

Furthermore, ethical issues can arise from cases that are not so mysterious in their origins. The question of why America bombed Hiroshima *and* Nagasaki may be presented as a mysterious question of motives, including everything from saving American lives to impressing the Soviet Union with the might of our new weapon. Yet as we have seen, you can also limit the complexity of the material and present students with a minor mystery about dropping the bomb. The moral dimensions of dropping the bomb on a civilian population, even if we accept as a premise that it was only to save the lives of American soldiers, is still infinitely complex.

*Jack*: Slow down. You think the bombing proves something, but I never said moral problems could not arise from straightforward historical situations. My point is the opposite, that you cannot have a truly complex historical mystery absent a value problem.

*David*: Now that you are limiting your claims, we are getting somewhere. History *can* be very mysterious when there is something important that can't be solved with the available evidence. There *may* be value issues as well, but a major mystery can arise from missing data too. And it can arise from conflicting data, from multiple perspectives, especially if these are mutually exclusive rather than complementary. It could be very difficult to sort out causes and consequences in an historical situation, let's say of combatants, if no one agrees on the basic story. Osama Bin Laden is the pinnacle of evil in one part of the world and a great leader and exemplar in another part of the world. How do we reconcile perspectives that are so very different? The morality of Bin Laden's bombing is not so complex, but the historical issue here is a very difficult mystery, don't you think?

*Jack*: Missing data is more of a puzzle. The puzzle can be very difficult if there are a lot of missing pieces and the pieces have been all mixed up or partly destroyed. However, that is more of a detective piece, a whodunit, not a *whydunit*. And, just to add a point, if you think the bombing of the WTC on September 11th was not so complex an event, I think you are completely wrong about this. . . . It is only from a purely American point of view, simplified by the press and government that this can be seen as a simple attack by evil parties seeking to destroy our nation . . . there is a lot more to it than that, and the *other side* has what it sees as a *moral* position of its own, however much we hate it.

*David*: Well, a whodunit that is complex and rich and full of errors and comprehension problems can be very effective with students, although we are short of the big major questions that you pose. But minor mysteries and medium mysteries can be mighty satisfying, and even here we need to sharpen our distinctions, improve our definitions. Furthermore, historical mysteries are not exactly like murder mysteries, in my view, but just as interesting. Lots of times, it doesn't matter who did it, or with what weapon, or where or when. Sometimes, it is much more interesting to learn about the different conclusions of historians and observers about their interpretations of the event. That can tell you as much about *their* times as the event did about its own era. And getting into the heads of people who lived in the past is a major mystery, even if it does not call for a value judgment.

*Jack*: Well, there I agree with you. Perspective and corroboration are interesting mysteries no matter where or when you find them, including the very present which is filled with problems of perception and interpretation from governments on down to the *person in the street*. Everyone has views, and these often don't agree with each other, or overlap, or contradict one another. This is a basic historical dilemma.

*David*: And it is the dilemmas, conundrums, conflicting interpretations, and clashing views that produce historical mysteries that force us to make choices and reexamine our own views of people, places, and events.

*Socrates*: Perhaps you are both correct. Perhaps you are both misleading yourselves. You should reflect on your own beliefs in order to determine which may stand up to reason. Evidence supports reason, but reason is not solely dependent on evidence. History may be studied as accounts of the Golden Age, the Past as satisfying mythology, possibly far more satisfying than the history of current reality. Mysteriousness, as the Oracle of Delphi once pointed out to me during a friendly argument, is essential to human development. It is a necessity, not simply a pleasure. A good story, as the Oracle knew, could change the fate of history. My friend Plato's cave may, for example, be a much more pleasant place than we once considered it. Images, myths, and imagination, as well as literature in history, are at least as attractive as evidence written or drawn by those present who are subject to the whims of their cultures, politics, and personal egos. Their stories are history, but may not improve us. After all, must history be in pursuit of truth, of virtue, or of story? Must a choice be made?

*Jack and David*: Thank you, Socrates, for the (almost) last word on history as mystery!

---

### You Decide

- What do you think is the priority goal for history: *Truth*, *virtue*, or *story*, or all?

- Maybe you don't want to choose? If not, explain why not. If so, write your own Socratic Dialogue with yourself or a colleague or friend, and settle the matter. Please!

---

## Building a sense of mystery

In this book, we have attempted to provide you and ourselves with a framework for teaching history as mystery. We interpret mystery in history broadly to include situations where there really are mysteries all the way to situations where mysteries have to be *manufactured* or *constructed* by us to provoke student interest. Above all, we maintain that the concept of mystery is inherently, psychologically, motivating to people and students—at least those of us who have not had our natural-born curiosity crushed by the demands of modern life and too much coverage and testing. Mysteriousness is especially fascinating to the young and the inexperienced, and if carried out cleverly in a classroom, gives competition to *X-Files*, Sherlock Holmes, Dashiell Hammett, and other fictions, past and present.

The real thing can be just as much of a mystery as the dramatic fiction we enjoy watching and reading. The biggest and most important art that a teacher can perform when presenting a mystery in history is to hold off on the answers, to let the data speak, to give the students the chance to develop their own interpretations, and to build an atmosphere of uncertainty and puzzlement. That's the *ticket* to interest and fascination with history, don't you agree?

## A review of cases and examples

This book has been devoted to developing a strategy of mystery in the teaching of history, with most of our examples coming from U.S. history. We have used examples from history dating back to prehistoric times (i.e., the drawings at Fossum) through Jefferson and Hemings to the American Old West on up to fairly recent events such as the Vietnam conflict. In between, we have presented some case studies and several smaller tidbits of data and examples that you can use to whet students' appetites for solving problems and discussing historical evidence.

We presented a case study from the Vietnam War as a problem of weighing and sorting evidence from a tense political situation, one where conflicts produced what were likely manufactured reports used to justify military action.

Thomas Jefferson's two families served us well as a study in the use of both historical and scientific evidence, and as a wonderful case study in competing values and biases that has lasted up to and including the present day. Issues and problems in history have a way of continuing as baggage long after the people and events have been consigned to textbooks as seemingly dead and final. Our friends Calamity Jane and Annie Oakley, representing outstanding Western women, are two lives that intertwine myth and history, make-believe and reality, in ways that call on us to question just how stories are born and communicated. These women from the story of the Old West raise questions about image and reality, and whether it is possible to separate facts from imagination, truth from invention, myth from reality, particularly as time moves forward. Overall, as we hope you agree, we have attempted to vary the historical period, the type of concept that is central to our inquiry, the problem-solving strategy, and the level of mystery.

## Central concepts in teaching history as mystery

Throughout, we have focused on a few central concepts that we believe are rooted in the process of historical understanding for all students and teachers. These central concepts or ideas are: perspective/viewpoint, concordance, mythmaking, bias, evidence, and interpretation.

We maintain that any and all study of history will evoke one or more of these concepts because problems, questions, and inconsistencies are embedded in any event. Witness accounts are sometimes clear but sometimes confusing, and artifacts can provide us with important clues, but also may offer puzzling features that are difficult to interpret. There are nearly always issues in the reports of witnesses and historians—even those who have studied a topic in depth—that may still be subject to the pressures and beliefs of the times, or to individuals' personal theories and biases. History can be very conflicted, confusing, and incomplete with firsthand evidence, which is the basis for all future interpretation, in need of considerable organization and "cleaning" for us to use. The process of making history takes a lot of study and editing.

Students, by contrast, frequently learn history as information that has been processed, packaged, edited, and summarized for them in a way that precludes direct contact with the messy, partial, and inconsistent materials on which a finished text is based. It is a lot like finding a nice clean stamped chicken body washed and packaged in the supermarket, without realizing that this was once a living creature with feathers, a head and a tail that walked around a barnyard. Therefore this book has been devoted to offering you and your students some case study materials that afford direct contact with evidence and with the interpreters of evidence. The evidence that we have presented clearly is often insufficient, subject to bias, and/or may even provoke controversy. The interpreters, even historians who are very professional, can fall prey to their own prejudices and viewpoints, fail to take into account the view of others, or be blind to the nature of the available evidence. Basically, what we are trying to say, and have already said many times over in many different ways, is that history can always be reviewed and rewritten. We hope you agree that there is always room for new interpretations, and new evidence often turns up to change our views.

## Taking another look at the minor, medium, and major levels of mystery

Mystery in history, in our view, has been defined as a process of seeking out unknowns, completing puzzles, comparing and contrasting viewpoints, solving problems, and trying to settle conflicts. Levels of mystery have been derived largely from the complexity and mix of these problems, but we are still debating just how to classify the examples we have presented, as well as those encountered in a typical American or global history program in any school.

We have offered a classification scheme for mysteries as minor, medium, or major, which we have applied with some, but not total success, to our examples: the Vietnam War, Jefferson's families, and Western women. We have provided you with our judgments, as well as invited you to argue with us and to develop and express your own judgments.

In our view of teaching history, a sense of mystery can be communicated by a teacher through many and varied methods. One prominent method is to present history as a series of puzzles, with the missing pieces being parts of the data. This we have generally termed a minor mystery because it mainly involves concerns about the quantity and quality of the primary evidence. But, the minor qualities can quickly grow into medium or possibly major issues if we begin to look at the historical bias toward Native Americans, and at the ways in which early interpreters made serious errors in the way they approached archeological evidence. We might conclude that their biases, reflecting the popular views of their time, were poorly adapted to view a *foreign* culture from the ancient past with any degree of objectivity. In effect, we are beginning to question the reliability of witnesses, and if presented with several disagreements, we have a rather complicated corroboration study to work out. Thus, in classifying mysteries, much depends on the nature of the evidence and what sorts of problems we are seeking, as well as the theoretical or conceptual perspective we bring to the problems.

A second important way to present history is as a set of accounts that have been written from different viewpoints. We have usually called multiple-viewpoint cases medium mysteries because their *solution* involves a good deal of corroboration work. Viewpoints can be complementary or conflicting, each raising its own set of questions. Viewpoints may also be confusing, with witnesses expressing inconsistent and mixed recountings or changing perspectives. This level of medium mystery can easily slide into a bigger problem if we add images and documents from unreliable or hostile witnesses who basically made up stories, used images for propaganda purposes or financial gain, invented outright lies, and/or created myths about themselves and others. By the time motives and mythmaking are added to multiple viewpoints, we are approaching a major mystery level that will call on students to deal with fairly difficult questions.

A third way of classifying mysteries in history is to focus on the context itself, its beliefs and theories, both for the witnesses and the professional historians and social scientists. Once interpretations are involved in a study, with collations of primary and secondary multiple accounts, including the values and biases of the times in which evidence was collected, we are probably in major mystery territory. When views and context have been overlooked, or accepted as fact without considering the orientation and consciousness of the historians doing the storytelling, we have entered a major mystery in which the past is covered by well-developed interpretations that may disguise or misdirect understandings from other viewpoints. For example, much of history has simply ignored gender, or the views of the conquered, or those at the bottom of the social ladder. Once outsider accounts or pictures are added into the equation, our conclusions about an event or person can change dramatically.

In addition to these different ways of looking at history as mystery, we might add that history scholars are also part of the problem of determining objectivity and reliability. They (and we) are prone to the same prejudices and *in* theories that the rest of us believe, only they are communicating the story to the public *and* to posterity! Thus, as you can see, there are plenty of opportunities for teaching history as *major* mystery because history often is deeply and satisfyingly mysterious. Even when evidence is discovered that solves a mystery, there are other problems that arise—problems of interpretation, suppression of information, political sensitivities—issues of virtue, as Socrates might say.

## Cooking up mysteries

In this book we hope that we have provided both a formula for creating historical mysteries for the secondary classroom and an exploration of the meaning history and mysteries can hold. Since both of us like to cook and we have already used one metaphor, *mystery*, for much of the book, we would like to use *cooking*, culinary arts, as a means of thinking through some issues about how we constructed the book. There are aspects here that are like a take-out meal. We have worksheets and a number of documents that are, we hope, "ready to go." We have done our best to classroom-test these, and we have discussed a number of strategies for using them in the classroom. In the second chapter, we provided a mini-mystery on the Gulf of Tonkin that was developed and tested specifically for this book.

There are times when, as much as we enjoy cooking, we simply do not feel like it tonight, and this is true in our teaching as well. Besides, we may want to try a new cuisine at someone else's hand before we attempt to cook it ourselves, or get take-out just to find out if we like that kind of food at all. It can also be a luxurious experience to sit at the beach or in the park and spread out a meal we could never have prepared and packed ourselves and still gotten there after all. Maybe *take-out* is not the right analogy: Maybe we are inviting you over for a home-cooked meal. Tell us how it tastes and how your kids like it.

While there are several meals here, we hope that we have also provided some tasty recipes. Like the author of any cookbook, we would like to pride ourselves on giving clear directions that allow you to produce historical mysteries in your classroom that will look as appealing as the mysteries depicted in this book and that are as "tasty" as those we tried ourselves with our students. Clarity and direction require us to develop categories and classifications. So we produced the three levels of mystery and the five sliding scales for judging mysteries. Of course, we do not believe that there are three levels of mystery *out there* in the world, right next to the Bill of Rights or the bird on that ledge, no more than there are flames that are high, medium, or low. And we know that it takes different amounts of time to sauté an onion depending on your stove and your pan and how you sliced that onion.

As idiosyncratic as stoves, pans, and ovens are, classrooms (once you fill them with students and teachers) are "uniquer"! So we find that our rating scale works, that it seems to be something that helps us understand what we are constructing in the classroom, and that our students and colleagues find useful when we work with them on mysteries they are constructing. Like any recipe it is just a guideline, and of course you have to be the one who judges when your onions are soft, or when they are finally caramelizing—you cannot rely only on the estimate of how many minutes it *should* take. We have tried to be pretty clear about this. For instance, in our first discussion of the Jefferson/Hemings mystery, when we used five rating scales to assess each of the eight items of evidence, we suggested that the family trees could have been discussed under *Reliability* as easily as under *Comprehension*. That discussion, we hope, illuminated what we intended the categories to mean and gave you an idea of what comprehension we are looking for when we use that term.

After you have followed the recipe a time or two, or perhaps even the first time you use it if you are a comfortable and experienced chef, we expect that you will develop your own preferences and begin to improvise and change things around. At that point you will have moved from a cookie-cutter approach to a level of comfort with this type of cuisine. Learning to create and investigate historical mysteries in the classroom is similar to discovering new cuisine. First you try something prepared by someone else and, if you decide you like it, you get that cookbook. You look through it and discover some of the new spices you might be using, some new equipment you might need, and even new combinations of old foods you have used forever. You try something simple and stick close to the recipe, looking at the cookbook to be sure you are getting it right, and are aware that it might not taste great the first time you make it. But after a while, you flip through the cookbook, sometimes just to be sure you remember all of the ingredients or the steps, and other times to look for elements from different recipes that you would like to combine, this time using the mango salsa with the spicy chicken.

We hope that this book allows the same progression, from using some premade manufactured mysteries, to using our three levels and five ratings, to our rules for presenting mysteries to preparing your own, finally bringing you to the point at which you can put together mysteries following your own variations. Like any cookbook authors, we hope that you send us some of your recipes, tell us what doesn't work, and best of all, invite us to come cook with you—invite us into your classroom to enjoy a mystery of yours. There is always a need for high-quality and adaptable classroom materials, particularly ones that are not just geared to help students learn about a particular topic, ones that help students engage in learning the discipline of history and related social sciences as well.

The point is, however cut-and-dried a cookbook is, you can also use if for much more personal complicated culinary arts, not just follow a recipe for an instant class. Only take-out, basically the work of another person, can be consumed *as is*, but we are never really sure how it was prepared or what the original ingredients were while we eat the food. If we could produce a series of classroom-ready, high-quality mystery units, we would, and we would know that they can be endlessly adapted and reused. We still use some of the ancient Amherst or D.C. Heath teaching units from the 1960s, when we can get our hands on them, because these are engaging investigations that everyone needs as models for interesting historical research that combines both primary and secondary sources.

Like any cookbook, we hope you use our ideas and case studies many times to produce wonderful mysteries for your classroom. We think a recipe is not chef-proof and a curriculum is not teacher-proof. There are all kinds of things that can go wrong with the processes of both teaching and cooking that are bound to affect the results. Your attention can wander, you burn an ingredient, a key ingredient is missing, or your guests come late, turning a hot and delicate confection into a soggy, lukewarm mess. (Perhaps that is why we enjoy opening a bottle of wine or beer before we start cooking!) As we grow more expert with culinary and teaching skills, and learn how to interpret and adapt recipes and rules, we all develop different and higher levels of process skills.

## Epigrams and homilies in thinking about historical mysteries

> There may be more than one right answer, many answers, but there can still be some wrong answers as well.

> Understanding evidence is not simply a matter of splitting the difference between two different points of view; after all, one may be wrong and the other right, or both incorrect.

> It is not a matter of one historian being wrong and the other right. History and historiography keep on going. Almost nothing is final. A right answer in history is not a final answer. But we can still say something is very probably *right* or *wrong* in our more positivistic moments.

Primary and secondary sources are both worthy of our questioning. Primary sources give us access to the original evidence, and provide us with the ability to make independent judgments but there is so much material that we are always presenting a sampling rather than a complete package. A sampling of the Jefferson/Hemings data, for example, without the Madison Hemings memoir is a lot less valuable standing alone, but still allows us to formulate hypotheses about the case. A teacher's problem is always one of balance: How much to give that stimulates student thinking, usually a very modest amount; but also, how much to give overall up to the point of surfeit and boredom.

A secondary source may be horribly flawed, but it may also be more balanced than any single primary source. As historians and educators, we usually go to the secondary sources first to see what primary sources to look at. With students, it is often the other way around. We can give them the primary source first as the path into a case or historical event or person. Once they have wrestled with making meaning from it, we can ask them to look at secondary sources. We hope we have helped you to build a new attitude toward the study of history as somewhat unfinished and uncertain. We have argued that history should be viewed as open to interpretation, a subject for new and revised storytelling, or perhaps affirmation of *old* stories. Teaching history as a mystery ought to be managed in a way that invites serious yet playful detective work. We have argued that you should view the past as negotiable and open to new viewpoints and interpretations rather than frozen in time and space.

As you saw in the Jefferson/Hemings case, new evidence can turn up that proves or solves a mystery, or stimulates new interpretations. However, new interpretations can also be invented by reviewing old evidence—showing it off in a new light. Thus, Western Women and the Vietnam War can benefit from a review of previous theories and factual accounts, and these may yield some surprisingly new conclusions.

## *David and Jack duke it out*: Act II

*Socrates*: As I have pointed out many times, it is the dialog that counts not so much the data. My friend Herodotus would not have agreed since for him the story was supreme. He saw himself solely as an historian.

*Jack*: Well, I like a good story. But how do you see yourself?

*David*: I like a good story too, but how do we know it is true or not? Trust and truth are important, else how do we understand history?

*Socrates*: Does it matter? Isn't it more fascinating if the story is itself a mystery to fathom? Separating the true from the untrue is a great exercise in reason, one that we all need to practice else we shall all be fooled. And there need not be definitive solutions, such as those enjoyed by the weak-minded. I see myself as an historian, philosopher, gadfly, and challenger of poor logic, all together, and I question my own ideas and knowledge as well as those of others. That is much fairer than being the Authority.

*Jack*: That's a very good point and encourages the individual to think for herself or himself, judging the data and the arguments by established criteria, not the word of others, especially those who are in authority.

*David*: Every person is her or his own historian, is that what you are saying? Or is every person a mystery writer too?

*Jack*: I don't actually think there is a lot of difference between history and story, since all accounts, and tales have to be judged by some means, and always partly through our subjective experience, which is biased and full of errors.

*David*: Are you saying then that mysteries lie within most or all of history?

*Jack*: Well, yes, in different amounts and forms . . .

*Socrates*: Yes, when I taught the young folks sitting in a square in Athens near the Temple of Athena, Goddess of Wisdom, I tried to get them to make their own interpretations of the facts and the rules laid down by their elders, leaders, and priests. This was a necessary skill for people who would soon command our democracy. If all is settled, then how can anyone make a new judgment?

*Jack and David*: So you see change comes out of struggle and investigation, not simply knowing, or accepting . . .

*Socrates*: Exactly, but of course you must accept a good deal of hard work as your lot, and often social disapproval as well. People love mysteries but not always if they challenge the given wisdom. That is what I have learned at great cost, if you know the story and the mystery of the hemlock.

—Curtain—

So, let's hear it again for teaching history as mystery, whether through *real* mysteries, purposely constructed classroom problems and issues, or thought-provoking questions. Let's give a cheer or two for perplexity and puzzlement, values and virtues, as well! And, like our imaginary Socrates, let's be humble enough, honest enough, and fair enough (good values indeed!) to question our sources, our thinking, and our biases before making historical decisions.

## Additional Resources

### Books and Articles

BROWN, C. S. 1994. *Connecting with the Past: History Workshop in Middle and High Schools*. Portsmouth, NH: Heinemann.

EDINGER, M., AND FINS, S. 1998. *Far Away and Long Ago: Young Historians in the Classroom.* York, ME: Stenhouse.

GALT, M. F. 1992. *The Story in History: Writing Your Way into the American Experience*. New York: Teachers and Writers Collaborative.

KOBRIN, D. 1996. *Beyond the Textbook: Teaching History Using Documents and Primary Sources*. Portsmouth, NH: Heinemann.

LEVSTIK, L., AND BARTON, K. C. 1997. *Doing History: Investigating with Children in Elementary and Middle Schools*. Mahwah, NJ: Erlbaum Associates.

WEIZMANN, D. 1975. *My Backyard History Book*. Boston: Little, Brown.

ZARNOWSKI, M. 1998. "Coming Out from Under the Spell of Stories: Critiquing Historical Narratives." *The New Advocate* 11: 345–56.

ZEVIN, J. 2000. *Social Studies for the 21st Century: Methods and Materials for Teaching in Middle and Secondary Schools*. Mahwah, NJ: Erlbaum Associates.

### Key Websites

We recognize that all of the specific web addresses may have changed by the time this book is published. They have certainly changed since we started compiling the list. Usually searching for an organization by name on Google (*www.google.com*) will get you to their site, then searching the site will let you find the page you need. This is an idiosyncratic collection of sites, which we have found helpful in teaching through mystery.

*The National Park Service*: Teaching with Historic Places (TwHP) uses properties listed in the National Park Service's National Register of Historic Places to enliven history, social studies, geography, civics, and other subjects. TwHP has created a variety of products and activities that help teachers bring historic places into the classroom: *www.cr.nps.gov/NR/twhp/index.htm*

- National Parks main page for teachers and learners—*www.nps.gov/learn/*
- Effigy Mounds National Monument Teacher's Guide—*www.nps.gov/efmo /parks/*; the main website for Effigy Mounds is: *www.nps.gov/efmo/index.htm*

- Mesa Verde National Park Education Materials, Information, and Activities— *www.nps.gov/meve/mvnp/teacher/edlist.htm*

*Memory of the World: Directory of Digitized Collection*: *www.unesco.org/webworld/mdm/index_2.html*

*American Memory Collection at the Library of Congress Website*: *Memory.loc.gov/ammem/ndlpedu/index.html*; a page within the collection on using primary sources in the classroom is *http://Memory.loc.gov/ammem/ndlpedu/lessons/primary.html*

*EDSITEMENT*: The Best of Humanities on the Web from the National Endowment for the Humanities—*http://edsitement.neh.gov/*

*Jackdaw Publications*: A commercial publisher of primary document reproductions with an "original" feel that is fun in the classroom; it has a wide variety of useful historical topics—*www.jackdaw.com*

*Monticello*: The Home of Thomas Jefferson—*www.monticello.org/*

*The Media History Project*: A site for historians of communication, with rich content on media history: one goal of the site is "to encourage educators to train their students how to use the Internet, how to write for it, and how to report on it"—*mediahistory.umn.edu*

*National Archives and Records Administration*: Main page: *www.archives.gov/index.html*

*The Digital Classroom*: Main page for teachers at *www.archives.gov/digital_classroom/index.html*; see also page on Teaching with Documents, a series of teacher-written lesson plans revolving around primary source documents from the National Archives—*www.archives.gov/digital_classroom/teaching_with_documents.html*

*The Vincent Voice Library at The University of Michigan Library*: "Largest academic voice library in the nation"; some spoken-word materials are available online—*www.lib.msu.edu/vincent*

*Jamestown Discovery*: The Association for the Preservation of Virginia Antiquities' Jamestown Rediscovery archaeological project; Jamestown Rediscovery is investigating the remains of 1607–1698 Jamestown on the APVA property on Jamestown Island, Virginia—*www.apva.org/jr.html*

*Consider the Source: Historical Records in the Classroom*: From the New York State Archives—*www.archives.nysed.gov/services/teachers/cts/ctstoc.htm*

*History Matters*: Designed for high school and college teachers of U.S. history courses; this site serves as a gateway to web resources and offers useful materials for teaching U.S. history—*http://historymatters.gmu.edu/*

*National Center for History in Schools*: The National History Standards and many lessons—*www.sscnet.ucla.edu/nchs/*

*Reel History 1302 with Peter Myers and Irene Scharf*: A general survey of U.S. history from the post-Civil War era to the present; this team-taught course studies the American experience in interactive ways, using media, the Internet, and online and print information sources—*www.accd.edu/pac/history/hist1302/reelhs.htm*

*Soon's Historical Fiction Site*: "The proposed Historical Fiction Network website"— *http://uts.cc.utexas.edu/~soon/histfiction/*

*The Gilder-Lehrman Institute of American History*: Resources for teaching U.S. history, annotated primary sources, teacher institutes, and fellowships—*www.gliah.uh.edu /index.cfm*

*Working Films*: Resource for using documentary films in the classroom— *www.workingfilms.org/*

# INDEX